Help!
Someone I
Love is
Depressed

Advance Praise

THIS IS *SUCH* A NEEDED book! Its needed not only because of its topic but the book in particular is needed because it is so well written. I've read other books by individuals who have experienced depression and they have often been so poorly organized or so poorly researched or so poorly written or so esoteric that they depressed me.

The content is clear, authentic, personal, and written in a manner to which anyone who reads it can relate. It is brilliant - not in that it's presented as a textbook on depression - but it is brilliant in its accuracy and its clarity and its readability. It is an important book. It is one that I think God will really use both to help individuals understand depression and to show them how God can help with this problem.

All of the chapters are essential, exceptional, so much so that I'm not able to pull out the most "pertinent": from Greg sharing his story to unraveling the myths of depression (boy, those are 3 biggies, too!). I loved the discussion around "Pardon me, a demon from where?" - As well as his comparison of depression to leprosy, "Instead of dealing with cracked skin, the depressed individual deals with a cracked soul." The discussion of the big three: serotonin, norepinephrine, and dopamine are right on target, clear, and informative.

How true, "....the problem of depression is not the loss; it is the attachment to the loss." I also laughed at the stark truth behind the jest: "the army of the Lord is the only one in which they shoot their wounded." The 13th chapter on suicide is excellent. This book will go on my bookcase at home, repeatedly, as I give it as a gift each time I meet someone who is suffering from this horrible problem.

—Patricia Laster, Ed.D Psychology

Help! Someone I Love is Depressed

Practical insights for those who suffer through bouts of depression and their families, friends, caregivers, and churches.

Greg L. Russ

AMBASSADOR INTERNATIONAL
GREENVILLE, SOUTH CAROLINA & BELFAST, NORTHERN IRELAND

www.ambassador-international.com

HELP! SOMEONE I LOVE IS DEPRESSED

Practical insights for those who suffer through bouts of depression and their families, friends, caregivers, and churches

Printed in the United States of America

ISBN: 978-1-62020-206-7
eISBN: 978-1-62020-304-0

Author photo: Vickie Brock
Cover design & typesetting: Matthew Mulder
E-book conversion: Anna Riebe

AMBASSADOR INTERNATIONAL
Emerald House
427 Wade Hampton Blvd.
Greenville, SC 29609, USA
www.ambassador-international.com

AMBASSADOR BOOKS
The Mount
2 Woodstock Link
Belfast, BT6 8DD, Northern Ireland, UK
www.ambassadormedia.co.uk

The colophon is a trademark of Ambassador

I dedicate this writing to Miriam, my beautiful and persevering wife,
who has endured this difficult path, and stayed by my side.
I love you, Greg

More Advance Praise for Help! Someone I Love is Depressed

THE DECADES-OLD DISCONNECTION BETWEEN RELIGION and the treatment of mental illness is unfortunate and inhumane. Greg Russ' book does much to bridge that chasm. Mental illnesses are not reflections of weaknesses, character defects, or lack of faith, but are very real medical conditions.

As a member of the clergy and a survivor of depression, Russ brings a unique perspective to the recognition of mental illnesses, effectively de-stigmatizing those potentially life-threatening conditions. I strongly recommend his book for anyone of faith; it is an invaluable opportunity to understand the pain and suffering associated with mental illnesses, as well as the collaboration between faith, science, and common sense, all of which contribute to recovery.

— Dr. Jeffery K. Smith, senior partner of Piedmont Psychiatry, Greenville, SC and author of *Bad Blood: Lyndon B. Johnson, Robert F. Kennedy, and the Tumultuous 1960s*

HELP! SOMEONE I LOVE IS DEPRESSED is a compelling journey through the dark valley of the shadow of death and back into the light of God's grace. As I read Greg's book, I instantly realized this is no mere academic treatment on the subject of depression. Rather, Greg writes as one "who has been there." He does not describe the dark days of depression from a distance as one who has heard about it, but rather he has actually gone through the doubt-ridden, self-questioning, horrific experience of battling depression. Along the way, Greg has had to grapple with how the God and Savior he loves figures into the equation. Why must a godly man suffer? Greg offers unique insights that will help others battling depression find hope.

However, his book will do much more. For the pastor who ministers to people with depression, Greg provides a plethora of insights into understanding the way depressed people feel and think. The book is filled with scriptural references, a clue to Greg's answer to the role of God in the daily fight with depression. I recommend this book for those still in the valley and for those who care enough to minister to them.

—Dr Wayne VanHorn, Dean, School of Religious Studies,
Mississippi College

WE HAD RECENTLY RETURNED FROM the mission field where our dream of spending our life in Ecuador came crashing down due to complications with cholera. I was so discouraged in my spirit. I had been battling depression in my own secret world. When I met Greg, I asked him how his book would be different from every other book on depression. By the time our conversation ended, I felt a flicker of light in my spirit.

The book is written in a very personable manner. He brings all the physiological and scientific terms to a level that any reader can comprehend. It is a powerful tool for one battling depression, as well as, the one who is swimming upstream trying to carry a depressed person back to shore. I use his concepts over and over as I counsel with others. I would recommend this book to anyone longing to see the light again.

—Ruth McWhite, Women's Ministry Director,
North Greenville University

Contents

Dear Church:

Acknowledgements:

FOR THE THREE HUNDRED DEPRESSION sufferers I worked with, thank you. God has used your experiences to help flesh out the concepts on these pages. I want to thank my good friend, Dr. Jeffery K. Smith, for your dedication and expertise in mentoring me through this writing project. You gave me the gift of your time, to which I am forever grateful. Thank you Dr. Arch Hart for teaching me what God taught you about depression. It's a privilege to further your work! Thanks to Dr. Bobby Clinton, who wrote a "Special Blessing" for me on May 14, 1999, manifesting in the release of this book. Dr. Harold Bryson and Dr. Wayne VanHorn, thanks for your theological guidance. Thanks to Dr. Dwight Carlson for your good work on anger and the recommendations you suggested before the last rewrite. Dr. Bruce Hennigan, thanks for giving me permission to use your brilliant piece, "Sarah Who." Jon Glickman, thanks for your encouragement and wisdom. Cathy and Ruth, thanks for cheering me on all these years. Carole and Kathy, thanks for reading and rereading the manuscript. Thanks to Dr. Sam, Tim, Matthew, Vanessa and Anna at Ambassador International for making this book become a reality. Last, but not least, to all of you who have prayed, given financially for my education, and encouraged me to keep going, thank you!

May the LORD bless and keep each of you,

Greg

Introduction

AN INVITATION TO HELP PEOPLE EXPERIENCING DEPRESSION

I have survived five bouts of clinical depression. It is by God's *mercy* my life has been spared. The shared insights were born out of excruciating emotional pain, and have allowed me to help over three hundred depression and manic-depression (bi-polar) sufferers as I wrote my doctoral thesis.

Loved ones and friends can be taught to recognize depression (see chapter 14) and anxiety—the responsibility of nurturing depressed people need not remain solely in the hands of physicians, counselors, and therapists. The church, with appropriate guidance, can help brothers and sisters who suffer from depression and/or anxiety.

CONFUSING SOLUTIONS FOR DEPRESSION

Well-intentioned Christians often mistakenly view depression as a black and white issue, failing to consider gray areas. Individuals suffering with depression are told by some within the household of faith to trust God more, and/or pull themselves up by their bootstraps. The bootstrap method may work with situational depressions, but can contribute to worsening biologically-based mood disorders.

Biological depressions are physical illnesses, necessitating treatment with medications. However, medications alone are not the answer to treating depression—they surely are not cure-alls.

Ultimately, each individual must trust God for his or her well-being. As long as biological depressions are treated using situational solutions, and situational depressions are solely treated with biological solutions, the depression landscape will remain plagued by confusion and chaos.

A PROBING QUESTION

Is depression a demon from hell, modern-day leprosy, a chemical imbalance, or—having run its course—surprisingly, a deeper way of knowing God? This book will answer this question.

Depression is one of the most misunderstood illnesses in contemporary culture; for that matter, throughout the course of history. Depression is not a respecter of racial or socioeconomic boundaries; it affects people from all walks of life. President Abraham Lincoln said the following about his bout of depression:

> I am now the most miserable man living. If what I feel were equally distributed to the whole human family, there would not be one cheerful face on earth. Whether I shall ever be better, I cannot tell; I awfully forebode I shall not. To remain as I am is impossible. I must die or be better, it appears to me.[1]

Many people, including Christians, believe depression to be a form of punishment from God. Moreover, the term—depression

---

1   Robert E. Hales, Stuart C. Yudofsky, and John A. Talbott, *Textbook of Psychiatry,* 2nd ed. (Washington, D.C.: American Psychiatric Press, 1994), 468–69.

—confuses people. In an effort to fully understand my depression, I explored different points-of-view, offering practical wisdom gleaned from direct observation of my own and others' experiences.

Chapter 1

My Depression Journey in a Nutshell

AM I GOING CRAZY?

In February 1995, I apprehensively eased into a psychiatrist's office. Shame permeated my being from head to toe. It was the loneliest physical journey I had ever made. I thought I was going crazy and deeply fearful the doctor would confirm my self-diagnosis. The thought of failing my wife and our daughter, as well as my congregation, was overwhelming.

Sitting in the waiting room, my fear escalating, and then the psychiatrist called my name. After a thirty minute interview, he looked at me and said, "I have good and bad news. The good news is you aren't going crazy. The bad news is you're in severe depression."

This discussion was the beginning of my formal introduction to depression. Looking back, however, I realize my informal introduction had actually begun nine years earlier.

In 1986, I started a new job with United Parcel Service (UPS). It was a well-paid position, but also proved to be an incredibly stressful one. In spite of personal and professional successes, my life was soon dominated by horrific depression. The light of Jesus I had experienced for five years had suddenly disintegrated into a cloud of despair.

My mood was infiltrated with negative, dark thoughts; internal agitation was a constant companion. My appetite had disappeared, causing a twenty-two pound weight loss. I also experienced sleep deprivation for three months; I would dream about my UPS route all night, waking up sweating profusely.

When morning came, the stark reality of returning to work paralyzed me. My energy and motivation were non-existent. My lack of concentration; loss of pleasure; and feelings of isolation, self-doubt, loss of self-esteem, and social withdrawal had set hopelessness into motion.

Living with suicidal thoughts and obsessing over them is the nightmare of all nightmares. As my depression intensified, I twice contemplated suicide (*see* chapter 13).

On a cold, rainy day in early November, after my wife and our three month old daughter had left the house to run some errands, I seriously contemplated taking my shotgun and ending it all. It was the most frightful temptation I had ever experienced. Only God knows how I survived.

Perhaps, the words of Job saved me. Job 1:21 *(HCSB)* reads: "The Lord gives and the Lord takes away." I remember these words being present in the midst of the suicidal thoughts.

I considered medicine a sign of weakness and a lack of faith in God. However, because I had chosen to avoid doctors and medication, I came out of the depressive episode believing the entire experience was a punishment for my lack of faith.

In the fall of 1988, during a revival at my church, when the pastor preached from Isaiah 6:1–8, I felt God calling me into ministry full time. Divinely inspired, I left my job at UPS and entered college. After graduating from the University of South Carolina with a bachelor's degree, I was accepted at the New Orleans Baptist Theological Seminary. In 1994, I graduated with a master of divinity degree, and then I moved back to South Carolina.

In September 1994, I accepted a position as pastor of Enon Baptist Church in Easley, South Carolina. Within three months of beginning my first pastorate, depression returned a second time. As a newly anointed man of God, I tried to ignore the downward emotional spiral to focus on strengthening my faith. This particular episode, however, was more intense than the first one–I was once more paralyzed by despair.

My options were limited: abandon the ministry, commit suicide, or consult a psychiatrist. Eventually, I scheduled an outpatient appointment with a local psychiatrist who prescribed an antidepressant. After nearly six months, the depressive symptoms responded to treatment.

Emotionally, I was seriously wounded on the frontlines, but by God's miraculous grace, I made it through that year. Remarkably, my congregation was unaware of the severity of my condition.

More than ever, I was determined to fully understand what causes depression. Christian and secular scholars defined the root cause of depression to be anger turned inward. I tried to apply this understanding to my own life, but could not establish any practical application.

One day, as I listened to a radio broadcast of *Focus on the Family*, Dr. Archibald Hart, dean of psychology at Fuller Theological Seminary, discussed depression. He stressed the root cause centers around *losses* in one's life. Hart's theory made perfect sense to me, providing a valid entry point for my healing journey. I was moved to enroll at Fuller to further my studies under the guidance of Dr. Hart.

As I gained greater insight and pursued my doctoral education from the pastorate, two additional episodes of depression ensued in 2001 and 2003. The 2001 episode slowly emerged in late January. By March, I was in the midst of another full blown bout.

In May I was scheduled to fly to Pasadena to attend a two-week intense workshop with Dr. Hart entitled "Enhanced Counseling Skills."[2] Since others had funded the trip, I felt I had no choice, but to attend the seminar. I cried at the airport, wondering if I would ever make it home again.

Like previous depression episodes, the horrendous consideration of suicide became my close companion. This time, however, I was terrified by the sight of knives. My psychiatrist advised me for some people, being afraid of sharp objects was typical for more severe forms of depression. This insight did nothing to take away the horrid fear!

When I arrived at the Fuller guesthouse in California, I noticed a small steak knife in the kitchen drawer. My fear escalated; I knew I had to get rid of it. The next morning I put the knife in the trunk of my rental car.

For two weeks, I listened to lectures on every major mental illness known to man. I had to get up an hour early every morning to run around the block three times to generate enough exercise-induced endorphins to survive the day. The low point of my doctoral

---

2   "Enhanced Counseling Skills," Fuller Theological Seminary, Pasadena, CA, May 16, 2001.

experience came when I confided in Dr. Hart about hiding the steak knife.

When I made it back to Greenville, I went to my family physician. He informed me my diastolic (lower end) blood pressure reading was over one hundred. I often wonder how my body did not collapse on the sidewalk in Pasadena—from a stroke or heart attack—during those early morning runs.

By the mercy of God, I eventually finished my dissertation and graduated in April 2006. My clinical course, however, was complicated by my refusal to properly take my prescribed medication. Over time, I have come to accept the necessity of remaining medicated, knowing without appropriate treatment, depression invariably returns, paralyzing my life and halting my productivity.

Concerning my faith, I have embarked on a diverse journey from Catholic schoolboy to Baptist minister to disciple serving the Kingdom of God. It has taken me from one end of Christianity to the other. My hope is the words contained within the subsequent pages of this book will minister to everyone reading them, regardless of anyone's unique background.

The remainder of this book chronicles my journey to learn how to cope with depression, and how I became inspired to mercifully help others come to terms with their journeys.

Part I

Family, Friends, Caregivers, and Pastors:

A Look Inside Your Loved One's Depression

Chapter 2

Unraveling Depression Myths

COMPLICATING THE COMPLICATED

Embracing the myths about depression is much like pouring gasoline on fire. When an illness carries with it a societal stigma, such as depression, its myth is greatly enlarged. Such misconceptions distract us from the truth, which adds *insult* to injury. Myth is defined in *Merriam-Webster's Collegiate Dictionary* as: a popular belief or tradition that has grown up around something or someone.[3] Understanding myths, and having liberty to refute them, is life-changing.

There are numerous myths surrounding depression. Among the most common are: (1) depression is simply another name for being unhappy or sad about something, (2) spiritually-sound individuals do not need treatment for depression, and (3) antidepressant medications are nothing more than "happy pills." Embracing these three myths is what kept me in bondage for years.

Believers of the first myth mistakenly assert that depression

---

3 *Merriam-Webster's Collegiate Dictionary*. 11th ed. Springfield, MA: Merriam-Webster, 2003, http://www.merriam-webster.com/dictionary/myth.

is another name for being unhappy or "blue." In my early years of battling depression, I referred to my darkened moods as *blue*, rather than depressed. Differentiating sadness from depression was a major breakthrough in my recovery.

Sadness is a normal emotion or condition of the human experience. Most individuals experiencing sadness or the blues bounce back within a few days. Depression, a much more serious state-of-mind, is not synonymous with sadness or temporary blues.

Individuals must experience a number of symptoms, including deep sadness for at least two weeks, in order to meet the diagnostic criteria for major depression. Healthy people experiencing bouts of sadness, or the blues, are in a different league from people experiencing more severe situational or biological depression. In summary, mere sadness does not equate depression. Choosing to believe *my* depression was only a blue mood drove me deeper into the abyss.

The second myth suggests spiritually-strong people do not need treatment for depression. As a simple, but parallel example, imagine someone in an emergency room, experiencing a heart attack. What if the individual refused medical help, falsely believing they only need God? Such a response rejects the notion God chooses to work through healthcare practitioners. The rejection of mental health practitioners, counseling, and medications is thereby erroneous.

Dr. Hart points out the fallacy of equating depression with a lack of faith:

> The tendency on the part of some Christians to spiritualize all depressions is dangerous. This is a common theme in the

teaching of many popular preachers, and it has been around a long time.

Job heard that thought when God tested him with affliction. His friends tried to comfort him by asking, "Is not your wickedness great? Are not your sins endless?" (Job 22:5, NIV). Job had already responded, "Miserable comforters are you all!" (Job 16:2, NIV), and he was right! He knew he had not sinned and in the end, God vindicated him. But in between, he did suffer from depression.

Another common idea is that healing from depression is exclusively a spiritual exercise. Some preach and teach that all depression is healed by simply confessing it, repenting of it, and turning back to God. This idea fails to recognize that many of our depressions have roots in biochemical or genetic causes, or that a legitimate spiritual discipline needs to be exercised through our depressions. I am a strong believer that God can help us in the healing process and that when it's an entirely spiritual matter, He provides the healing. But in many instances, our depression needs help in addition to whatever prayer or confession we need to make.

As Christians we need to be open to God's miraculous interventions. There are times when He provides healing without any physical interference or psychological assistance. Many people, however, need to be pointed to the resources of the gospel and to see what they are doing in their personal lives that can be causing or perpetuating their depression.[4]

Everyone requires a measure of healing at some point in his or

---

4   Archibald D. Hart, *Dark Clouds, Silver Linings* (Colorado Springs: Focus on the Family, 1993), 108–109,

her life. Even spiritually-strong persons may experience depression and need treatment. Such individuals may have a greater need for healing because their denial of depression and rejection of help intensify the symptoms. Falling captive to this myth, I never sought treatment for my first bout of depression.

The third myth suggests antidepressant medications are just "happy pills." Many depressed people are told: "Anybody who takes pills for depression just needs to get a grip; you wouldn't need medicine, if you trusted God more."

Unfortunately, foolish pride perpetuates this myth. Humans are incredibly tenacious, thinking we can do it alone. Blinded by pride, I swallowed this myth hook, line, and sinker.

The good news is God often works through medications. Millions of people, who steadfastly trust in God, also take insulin and blood pressure medications. Antidepressant medications do not elevate the mood nor do they belong in the same category as potentially-intoxicating prescription medications and abusive street drugs. Antidepressants allow the depressed person to feel normal and do not change the individual's baseline personality.

Antidepressants were an accidental discovery in the middle of the twentieth century, as scientists sought a cure for tuberculosis. A particular anti-tubercular medication was coincidently discovered to lessen the symptoms associated with depression. God showered His grace upon the human race, allowing researchers to discover this medication by default. Antidepressants, when needed, are God's gift.

There are countless adjectives that portray the dark existence of the depressed individual. In the next three chapters, descriptive word pictures will be thoroughly used to examine the following question: is depression a demon from hell, modern day leprosy, a chemical imbalance, or having run its course, surprisingly, a deeper way of knowing God?

Chapter 3

Pardon Me, A Demon from Where?

A Demon from Hell

During the worst moments of my depressions, I truly felt demonized. The expression, "a demon from hell," symbolizes utter darkness, deep fright, and paralyzing fear.

Many people ask the question, "What is hell anyway?" Opinions are as varied as the seemingly endless spectrum of colors. Universalists do not believe in a literal hell. Some Christians think certain people are destined for eternal damnation, without a choice. Others think hell is a myth.

The Bible, however, describes hell as a very real place. Jesus uses very descriptive language when describing hell, often using the Greek word *gehenna*. Jesus quite often spoke in picture language.

In his book, *The Reality of Hell and the Goodness of God*, Harold Bryson says:

> He spoke of himself as the Vine, the Bread of life, the Light of the world, the Good Shepherd, the Door, and many other figurative expressions. He compared the relation of people

31

with him as branches. From the symbols we discover the truth they convey.

To understand the New Testament doctrine of hell we must learn something of the setting of the figures of speech used to describe it. An examination of the metaphorical languages leads one to conclude that the writers were saying that hell is a place of wastefulness, hopelessness, sinfulness, loneliness, and endlessness.[5]

I have never met a person suffering from deep emotional pain who could not identify, at least in part, with those word pictures. At the height of depression, Bryson's five metaphors are most applicable. A closer examination of these metaphors can be helpful to family, friends, caregivers, and pastors of those who are, in fact, depressed.

WASTEFULNESS

Hell is likened to wastefulness. The word *gehenna* refers to the Valley of Hinnom, located outside the walls of Jerusalem. It was there where Israel and her unfaithful kings burned their sons and daughters in honor of Molech. The memories of this horrendous behavior eventually led to this valley becoming a garbage dump for the city of Jerusalem.

This event portrays a vivid snap shot of depression, when the individual feels trapped in a garbage dump, wasting away. At the height of my depression, life—at best—felt like a wasteland: barren and cold.

---

5   Harold T. Bryson, *The Reality of Hell and the Goodness of God* (Wheaton, IL: Tyndale House Publishers, 1984), 48.

HOPELESSNESS

The second metaphor describes hell as a place of hopelessness. Hopelessness invariably leads to despair. Both conditions are depression's evil twin companions.

As Christians, God calls us to face our pain and sorrow honestly. In the midst of deep darkness, depressed individuals judge themselves as guilty. They passively declare themselves worthy of despair.

For those who have faith in Jesus, permanent despair has no rightful place in their lives. When befriending people through a bout of depression, this is a critical juncture. This distorted reality must be challenged and changed—the depressed person needs to know he or she, not God, has allowed despair to take root.

Just as they have learned to be hopeless and helpless, they can also relearn hopefulness and helpfulness. By the mercy of God, I am a living example of such a blessed recovery.

SINFULNESS

Sinfulness is the least surprising metaphor in the description of hell. Sin and hell are miserable, yet natural companions. The expressions "outer darkness" and the "weeping and gnashing of teeth" describe the horror of hell.[6]

In the Bible, the terms light and darkness are used to symbolize good and evil. Light is used to describe God, while darkness depicts sin. Jesus' coming is all about light illuminating darkness to rescue mankind from an eternity in hell (an eternal separation from God). Outer darkness does not describe an optical illusion, but a problem with sin, as evidenced in the words of Bryson:

---

6   Ibid., 53.

The human mind can hardly fathom either total light or complete darkness, which is why we cannot understand much about heaven or hell. The inhabitants of hell live in extreme selfishness. Selfishness makes us miserable and uncomfortable. It destroys interest in the welfare of others. The picture of "weeping and gnashing of teeth" is another picture of hell, expressing self-condemnation, self-loathing and misery. This may well refer to the gnawing pains of self-inflicted anguish eating away at the *vitals* of the soul. Christianity clearly teaches that after death personality survives. This means that when we leave this earth the only thing we take is ourselves.[7]

Depressed individuals clearly capture themselves in this snapshot! Depression thoroughly consumed my very soul, leaving me in utter despair.

LONELINESS

The metaphor of loneliness is very familiar to the depressed person. Loneliness is a constant companion during the depression journey. The mental condition involves intense feelings of being separated and alienated from God, and other meaningful relationships. Hence, rejection becomes a key player in the evolution of depression.

Depressed individuals can be around others, yet feel extremely lonely and isolated. Unconsciously, loved ones may intensify a depressed individual's sense of rejection and loneliness, by making flippant comments such as: "Just snap out of it," "Toughen up," "Be stronger," and so on. Those of us who have experienced depression must be taught our suffering is not in vain; the loneliness will one

---

7   Ibid., 51.

day give way to intimacy if we continue to follow Jesus through the healing process.

ENDLESSNESS

The last of the metaphors describes hell as endlessness. The Bible teaches hell is an endless, horrible existence, lasting for eternity. Depressed individuals believe their misery will never end, leading to an endless hell.

Catholics often describe purgatory—a place one goes after death—as a holding tank, providing the individual with one last opportunity to get right with God. Even though I do not believe in the existence of purgatory after death, I do agree with Larry Crabb, psychologist and author, who says a form of purgatory is present on Earth.

"We're not there yet. We sometimes experience, now, what seems like hell. But it isn't the hell of judgment; it's the hell of mercy, a kind of present purgatory."[8] Crabb suggests individuals, even in the height of their suffering (including depression), can experience the love and mercy of God even if they cannot feel it. I have no doubt Jesus protected and kept me in the midst of my "hell of mercy" journey!

Depressed people must learn to keep their eyes on Jesus, even when they cannot feel Him. As the depression clears, moving closer to Him will be much easier. His nailed-scarred hand, *holding my hand in the darkness* is, and will forever be, written on my heart.

Dark nights (demons from hell) often target Christians who appear most determined to follow Jesus. Those who God uses the most, often experience the deepest wounds.

---

8   Larry Crabb, *Shattered Dreams* (Colorado Springs: WaterBrook Press, 2001), 129.

Henri Nouwen, one of the finest spiritual writers of the twentieth century, described his own depression:

> That was a time of extreme anguish, during which I wondered whether I would be able to hold on to my own life. Everything came crashing down—my self-esteem, my energy to love and work, my sense of being loved, my hope for healing, my trust in God...everything. Here I was, a writer about the spiritual life, known as someone who loves God and gives hope to people, flat on the ground and in total darkness. I experienced myself as a useless, unloved, and despicable person. Just when people were putting their arms around me, I saw the endless depth of my human misery and felt there was nothing worth living for. All had become darkness. Within me there was one long scream coming from a place I didn't know existed, a place full of demons.[9]

Anyone who has ever experienced depression vividly recalls the horrors of those dark nights. Those afflicted with depression can identify with the metaphor of modern-day leprosy. We must next examine how to deal with this contemporary plague.

---

9   Henri Nouwen, *The Inner Voice of Love: A Journey through Anguish to Freedom* (New York: Harper Collins, 1996), xiii–xv.

Chapter 4

Modern-Day What?

MODERN-DAY LEPROSY

Life as an outcast is devastating and radically painful. During my depressive episodes, I felt like an outcast, and was convinced no one knew what I was going through. *Living death* became my home address.

Leprosy is often called "a living death" because of its many horrifying effects on the human body.[10] Without the proper treatment, people are often left hopelessly deformed. Severe depression is certainly a living death. Therefore, it is critical to have caring family members and friends who understand what suffering loved ones are going through during depression.

Leprosy, as documented in the Bible, describes more than one illness. The Hebrew word for leprosy refers to many types of skin diseases—Exodus 4:6 (Moses), Numbers 12:1–10 (Miriam), and 2 Kings 5:8–14 (Naaman) cite varied examples of leprosy.

Merriam-Webster's Collegiate Dictionary defines leprosy as we know it today:

---

10   American Leprosy Missions, *The Disease*. http://www.leprosy.org/LEPdisease. html, 1, (accessed March 27, 2006; page now discontinued).

A chronic infectious disease caused by a mycobacterium affecting especially the skin and peripheral nerves and characterized by the formation of nodules or macules that enlarge and spread accompanied by loss of sensation and eventual paralysis, wasting of muscle, and production of deformities.[11]

Judging from the definition, leprosy is a dreaded disease. Though it is a curable malady, citizens in many poor, third world countries continue to suffer from the debilitating illness due to lack of access to healthcare.

Leprosy was a grossly misunderstood disease, until 1873, when Dr. Armauer Hansen made a radical discovery: leprosy is caused by bacteria. Prior to that time, many believed the dreaded disease was a hereditary sickness, curse, or punishment for sin.

In many cases, depression is viewed through the same prism as seventeenth century leprosy. Scientific studies have shown depression is often hereditary. However, many Christians perpetuate the myth depression is a curse or direct result of sin.

Hansen's findings were indisputable; the misguided fears of supposedly well-meaning believers were laid to rest. Depression is also clearly medically-based. To view it as a form of punishment is a by-product of fear and ignorance. In Matthew 7, Jesus warns against premature judgment—those who condemn depressed individuals are casting sin-laden stones.

PARALLELS: PHYSICAL AND SPIRITUAL LEPROSY

Leprosy causes substantial damage to nerve conduction in the human body. Likewise, depression also causes interference in nerve

---

11   *Merriam-Webster's Collegiate Dictionary.* 11th ed. Springfield, MA: Merriam-Webster, 2003

conduction, affecting emotions and pain control. When depressed individuals talk about living in pain, it is quite literal.

Whereas the leprosy patient literally suffers from dry, cracked skin, the depressed person feels isolated in an arid, barren, emotional desert. Instead of dealing with cracked skin, the depressed individual deals with a cracked soul.

Proper perspective in life is critical. John 12:24 refers to a corn of wheat falling onto the ground. This verse has become near and dear to my soul because the corn of wheat has to crack so the trapped, yet more abundant life, can germinate!

EYES

Leprosy affects the eyes in several ways. Diminished sensation due to nerve damage and dry eyes, along with decreased tear production, make the individual vulnerable to severe eye damage.[12] Some experience painful conjunctivitis (red eye), when bacteria invade the eye. If unattended, leprosy can lead to loss of vision.

Spiritually, the same is true. An individual's eyes are a window into his or her soul. Depression is often easy to detect, especially in the eyes of the sufferer.

Paul says on this earth, we see through a glass darkly, implying our sinful natures keep us from seeing as clearly as God intended. On occasion, everyone views the world through a dark prism. Those who are depressed almost exclusively use the dark lens as their view finder. I often advise depressed people not to make any major decisions until their depression has run its course, such that the temporary state of diminished concentration and negative outlook does not alter their judgment.

---

12   Ibid.

HANDS AND FEET

Leprosy patients are instructed to inspect their hands and feet on a daily basis for cuts, blisters, and inflamed areas. The hands and feet become focal points to determine if the disease is worsening. It is important to teach depressed individuals the appearance of certain symptoms (i.e., sad mood, changes in sleep pattern and appetite) are focal points to determine if their depression is worsening.

In the darkness of depression, it is difficult for an individual to differentiate what he or she is thinking and feeling. One thing is certain; all feelings—positive, negative, and irrational—are triggered by thoughts. Depressed persons, however, can learn to modify their thinking and change their negative emotions.

In the more severe cases, there may be an 8–16 week window (or longer in profound depression) when the lack of motivation and concentration are so impaired. The individual may have difficulty modifying his or her negative thinking processes.

After the window of time passes, new, more positive thought processes can be learned. Renewing the thought process requires patience on the part of the patient, his or her family and friends, as well as the treating therapist.

Modern-day leprosy is a useful and vivid way to describe depression. Physiology plays a critical role in the biologically-based depression. The underlying cause can best be described as a chemical imbalance in the brain.

Chapter 5

A Light Show in Slow Motion

CHEMICAL IMBALANCE

Those who have not experienced a chemical imbalance leading to depression often seem confused by the term. The following verbal illustrations will hopefully make this term more understandable.

Inside the human brain, an electric light show occurs twenty-four hours per day. The key players in the physiological show are chemicals known as neurotransmitters. Serotonin has often been referred to as the king of all neurotransmitters.

In author Bruce Hennigan's book *Conquering Depression,* he wrote at length about serotonin, calling it: Sarah Who:

> Let me introduce you to one of my medical school professors: Dr. Molly Cule. She has taught biochemistry, the study of biological chemicals, for years. An unusual teacher, Molly Cule, will inundate us with facts and figures, concentrations of this chemical and that enzyme, until we will be overwhelmed. With a twinkle in her eye, she feigns horror that we will be unable to take in any more information.

"Allow me to give you some advice", she says. 'You will forget 90 percent of everything you learn in medical school. But don't worry, you really only need about 85 percent of what you learn. Don't waste your time memorizing this minutiae I am doling out. For instance, who cares if the average goldfish gill mitochondria contains fourteen milligrams of serotonin? Ooops!'

She places her hand to her mouth in horror. 'I've just wasted another one of your neurons. You only have a certain amount, so don't waste neurons on meaningless facts you'll forget right after the next test. Save the neurons for the important facts that can help your patients.'

(This lecture actually happened years ago, and to this day I still recall that the average goldfish gill mitochondria contains fourteen milligrams of serotonin. My first introduction to this brain chemical came on a day I wasted a neuron!)

Serotonin. If you haven't heard about this neurotransmitter by now, you will hear more about it as you battle depression. It is a buzzword on all the television talk shows and pops up frequently in tabloid and magazine articles about depression. Most of the newer antidepressant medications work by their effect on serotonin levels in the brain. Serotonin is so important in understanding and overcoming depression that I would like to discuss it briefly and perhaps use up a few of your neurons.

Let's begin by joining Dr. Molly Cule in the biochemistry lab and see what we can learn about serotonin. Our professor is holding a model of two nerve endings very close to each other. Remember the synapse (the point at which a nerve impulse is transmitted from an axon of one neuron to the dendrite of another) we talked about on our voyage into the brain? As Dr. Cule introduces a chemical substance into the gap between the nerve endings, we see the spark of a nerve impulse jump from one nerve ending to the next. The chemical facilitating the nerve impulse conduction across the synapse is called a neurotransmitter.

Molly Cule is quick to point to a chart listing the benefits of neurotransmitters. They allow us to think, perceive, and move. Serotonin, the neurotransmitter we are most interested in, also controls the regulation of the contraction and expansion of blood vessels; the contraction of the 'smooth muscles' of our intestines that aid digestion by pushing food through the gastrointestinal tract; and the function of the 'platelets,' a component of blood that initiates blood clotting. So, without serotonin, the king of neurotransmitters, we wouldn't be able to survive very long.

Now Dr. Molly Cule is pointing to a diagram of the brain and its connections to the spinal cord. See the long set of nerve cells that extends from the brain all the way out to the body? These nerves are called the 'serotonin system,' and they extend from the brain to the body, composing the single largest system in the brain. This system influences a broad range of basic functions from movement to mood.

Aah, mood is what we are interested in! But did you catch that this system also affects movement?

You can appreciate how a loss of serotonin function can lower the mood and produce depression, as well as lower the movement throughout the body. This results in your feeling 'down' and at the same time having a loss of energy, increasing sleepiness, weight gain, and sluggishness. In fact, serotonin is only one of dozens of neurotransmitters that all have differing levels of effect. These numerous neurotransmitters work together in a system of checks and balances.

Now Dr. Molly Cule is pointing to a group of musicians waiting in the next room. You may want to cover your ears. It seems the musicians are all playing different songs. The sound is horrible! Dr. Cule saves the day by entering the room, rapping her baton on the podium, and taking control of the orchestra.

Whew! That's much better. Now all the musicians are playing the same song, at the same tempo, under the direction of our multitalented professor. As Thomas Carew, a Yale researcher, commented, 'Serotonin is only one of the molecules of the orchestra. But rather than being the trumpet or the cello player, it's the band leader who choreographs the output of the brain'.[13]

Hennigan's description of serotonin and its role in the human body is masterful and illuminating. Scientific studies show depleted serotonin levels are directly correlated with depression. One of serotonin's key roles is to balance normal mood variations. Biological depressions are caused by deficiencies in serotonin and other neurotransmitters, namely norepinephrine and dopamine.

When an individual resists treatment with an antidepressant medication, he or she is refusing a God-given opportunity to achieve recovery. If the depressed individual chooses to embrace God's gift, weakness can be transformed into strength (2 Corinthians 12:9).

---

13   Bruce Hennigan and Mark A. Sutton, *Conquering Depression: A 30-day Plan to Finding Happiness* (Nashville: Broadman and Holman Publishers, 2001) 90–92.

DEPLETED SEROTONIN DUE TO STRESS

Depletions of serotonin are directly linked to stress. The lifestyle of the twenty-first century is more stressful than ever, taxing both mind and body.

Dr. Hart clearly delineates the connection between stress and low serotonin levels (as documented in his best selling book, *The Hidden Link Between Adrenaline and Stress*)[14]. In Hart's opinion, "people were designed to move at the pace of a camel, but are instead moving at the pace of a supersonic jet."

Hart's words illustrate the hectic schedules so many of us follow. As serotonin levels decrease, the prevalence of depression rises.

Just as the pancreas of a diabetic patient is unable to produce enough insulin, the brain of a depressed individual lacks the capability to produce enough serotonin, norepinephrine, and/or dopamine. Having absorbed the pictorial language of the last three chapters, travel with me into Part II of this book as I share the insights God gave me to overcome depression, paving the way to know and experience Him in a deeper way. The journey begins at the intersection of *mercy* and *depression*.

---

14   Archibald D. Hart, *Adrenaline and Stress* (Nashville, TN: Word Publishing, 1995).

Part II

The Intersection of Mercy

and Depression:

A Journey Toward Progressive Healing

Chapter 6

Intersection Insights

DO THINGS REALLY WORK TOGETHER FOR GOOD?

The Scriptures tell us "all things work together for good to those who love God, to those who are called according to His purpose" (Romans 8:28, NKJV). However, following my first bout of depression, it was impossible for me to embrace such a possibility. When I contemplated the prospect of my suffering as a means by which I could establish a closer relationship with God, self-condemning, profane words instantly came to mind.

If anyone had suggested my misery could have positive consequences, I would have *wished* depression on him or her! Nine years later, my second major bout of depression occurred even more intense than my first episode. Eventually, I consented to taking an antidepressant medication which regulated my brain chemistry.

For the first time in ten years, I had a true sense of well-being. I realized I had been afflicted with a low-level depression between my two major bouts. Surprisingly, the Holy Spirit slowly began to show me how God was working through my depression.

The first insight was relatively simple, and proved to be the gateway to my recovery. A close examination of previous losses in my life became the focal point to begin the healing journey.

THE COMPLEXITY OF LOSS

Looking back, four major factors played contributory roles in my depressive episodes. The first factor was the array of losses in my life. Understanding the different facets of loss eventually became a valuable, emotional discipline for me. God gives us a life, which is more frail and temporal than most would admit. In the end, we lose everything that does not have eternal value, including our earthly bodies. Eventually, everyone must learn to deal with loss.

BEWARE OF GENERALIZATIONS

Examining loss in a generalized manner accomplishes very little. We must carefully and honestly analyze our personal losses. The personal insight gained from loss enriches our personality, and, subsequently, allows us to help others work through their losses.

Dr. Hart writes about the subject of loss with insightful clarity:

> In bereavement, the nature of our loss is well-grasped. This is why the grief of death, while painful, is essentially healthy. We know precisely what the loss is and that it is final. Our culture also gives us permission to experience our grief, and this helps us to accept the deep depression we feel as normal. This aids the grieving process.
>
> But it's not so easy to deal with life's lesser losses. Life's other losses are not easy to grasp, or to let go of. Getting fired from a job or being divorced by someone you still love is not a "clean" loss. Our grieving becomes confused and distracted by anger and resentment at what has happened to us, and our depression

becomes intense and even incapacitating. [15]

Hart taught four types of loss: real, abstract, imagined, and threatened. To help me better understand my losses, I divided them into four categories applicable for me.

1. *Actual Losses.* They exist in fact and are current. They usually involve the loss of something tangible—things we can see and touch. I get a speeding ticket. My daughter breaks her arm. My dog disappears. Actual losses are part of everyday life and are the easiest to deal with. We quickly feel the range of the loss, and usually, it is contained within boundaries we understand.

2. *Hidden Losses.* Baffling us, they are the hardest to grasp. They are made up of things we cannot see or touch: the loss of hope in a future dream, the loss of an individual's love or respect, the loss associated with failing at something important to us.

   It is helpful to see these hidden losses as creations of our minds. Their reality exists in our heads only. They are unique and will mean different things to different individuals.

   These losses may require another person to help us navigate through the complexity of the loss, allowing each individual to explore and discover what it means to him or her. Thinking through hidden losses by ourselves gets us nowhere. Often, all we do, is rehearse the loss over and over again.

---

15   15 Archibald D. Hart, *Unmasking Male Depression: Recognizing the Root Cause of Many Problem Behaviors, Such as Anger, Resentment, Abusiveness, Silence, Addictions, and Sexual Compulsiveness* (Nashville, TN: Word Publishing, 2001), 148.

3. *Dreamed-up Losses.* The imagination is a powerful force. Whereas actual losses are based on reality, these losses are not. At church, we think others are talking behind our back. When our grown children do not call or visit, we assume they are avoiding us. When our boss chooses another employee to complete a project, we think he or she is unfair. In our mind's eye, these losses are as powerful as the real ones—they put depression into motion just the same.

4. *Potential Losses.* These are life events that have the potential to become losses, yet have not yet occurred. A doctor orders more tests—we convince ourselves we have cancer. The company we work for loses an important account—we conclude a layoff is inevitable. Our car starts making a noise—we assume it needs a new motor.

We are threatened because these losses have the potential to occur, but in many cases, never do. All four categories of loss require different approaches for resolution. Many times a counselor or trusted friend is needed to help us make sense of the loss.

People can readily identify with the aforementioned losses. Part of the healing process is helping each person *activate* a strategy to cope with his or her loss.

Below are six steps I learned from Dr. Hart to recognize and deal with losses:

- Step One: Identify the Loss
- Step Two: Understand Every Facet of Each Loss
- Step Three: Separate the Different Types of Loss

- Step Four: Facilitate the Grieving Process
- Step Five: Face Up to the Reality of the Loss
- Step Six: Develop a Perspective About the Loss

I want to illustrate the above steps with a concrete example. When my oldest daughter was in elementary school, I would pray with her on the way to school, tell her I loved her, and give her a kiss. The school's front door was not far from the drop-off point, so I could sit in my car and watch her walk through the doors. She would always turn around and wave at me, before entering the building. I came to cherish that daily wave!

A few years later, on the first day of middle school when she got out of the car, she never looked back. At first, I attributed her standoffishness as a by-product of her desire to act mature among her peers. Unable to adjust to her newfound independence, I felt a creeping sadness.

By this time, I had already experienced two depressions, and knew all to well, that extended sadness did not show up to say hello. It had to be coming from a loss!

Step One: Identify the Loss. My daughter stopped looking back to wave.

Step Two: Understand Every Facet of Each Loss.

- She was in a new environment,
- Moreover, it was middle school, where the opinion of her peers carried greater weight,
- She was taking her first steps toward moving from childhood to adolescence, and
- I never realized how much her wave meant to me.

Step Three: Separate the Different Types of Loss.

- The *actual loss* was her moving into a new phase of her young life.
- The *hidden loss* was the loss of intimacy represented by the daily wave.
- The *dreamed-up loss* was thinking she did not want to look back and wave.
- The *potential loss* was my fear her friends were more important to her than her father.

Step Four: Facilitate the Grieving Process. In Matthew 5:4 (NKJV) our Lord says "Blessed are they that mourn, for they shall be comforted."

I am convinced God wants us to honestly grieve through our losses, regardless of their seeming insignificance. Having knowledge of the first four steps would be of no value if I had not given myself permission to grieve.

Step Five: Face Up to the Reality of the Loss. The wave that meant so much to me was now past tense. Now, I had to confront the loss, head on.

Step Six: Develop a Perspective on the Loss. In that setting, it is perfectly normal for someone her age to establish independence. She was totally unaware her actions had led me to feel sad and unwanted. I was forced to understand there would be plenty of opportunities to build intimacy in subsequent phases of her life.

Working through the above-referenced steps generates insight into the meaning of loss. Within a day or so of working through these steps, the gripping sadness dissipated. Such insights provide a valid entry point for developing and activating emotional skills (disciplines) essential to dealing with loss.

Another factor magnifying loss is our tendency to overly embrace people, places, and objects. Hart offers an interesting perspective on the attachment process in reference to loss:

> We can accept our losses with less pain and depression, if we will learn how to let go of our attachments. We humans are remarkably tenacious. For reasons of security or just plain hoarding, we do not let go very easily. When we love, we also want to possess; when we want something we desire, it becomes an obsession. Because we cling to possessions, ideas, reputations, and people, we experience losses very deeply, and the ensuing depressions are unnecessarily painful and prolonged. I repeat: the problem of depression is not the loss; it is the attachment to the lost object. We simply won't let it go![16]

For me, the key to understanding and accepting the detachment process is submitting to the Holy Spirit's guidance. He gives me the strength and mobility to detach from unwanted objects I hold tightly and, in turn, attach to the forgiveness and loving acceptance of Jesus Christ.

Upon completing an overview of the losses in one's life, and working through them, an individual can help others do the same. Understanding and dealing with loss neutralizes the first major underlying factor contributing to depression.

---

16   Archibald D. Hart, *Unmasking Male Depression: Recognizing the Root Cause of Many Problem Behaviors, Such as Anger, Resentment, Abusiveness, Silence, Addictions, and Sexual Compulsiveness* (Nashville, TN: Word Publishing, 2001), 138.

Chapter 7

Sanity Please

THINKING PATTERNS

Severe disturbances in our thought content and processes are often mislabeled as insanity. As I eventually discovered, thought disturbances accompany depression, which led me to research the biblical concept of sanity.

Eugene Peterson, author of *The Message,* introduces the proverbs, stating:

> Many people think that what's written in the Bible has mostly to do with getting people into heaven—getting right with God, saving their eternal souls. It does have to do with that, of course. But it is equally concerned with living on this earth—living well, living in *robust* sanity. In our Scriptures, heaven is not the primary concern, to which earth is a tag-along afterthought. "On earth as it is in heaven" is Jesus' prayer.[17] (emphasis mine)

The first time I read this quote, the possibility of attaining "robust sanity" leapt in my heart! I remember mulling the question:

---

17   Eugene H. Peterson, *The Message: The Bible in Contemporary Language* (Colorado Springs: Navpress, 2002).

what does *robust sanity* look like?

Proverbs 23:7 (NKJV) came to mind, "For as he thinks in his heart, so *is* he." This verse teaches us we are what we think, and thoughts lead to feelings (emotions), which generate behavior. To change an individual's emotional responses, it is essential to examine how he or she thinks.

According to Peterson, "robust sanity" should be the attainable baseline a disciple of Christ desires to experience. Other Scripture passages illustrate the plight of severely depressed individuals (Psalm 88:8), and the need to correct negative thinking (2 Corinthians 10:3–5).

During my depressive episodes, I had 8–16 week windows when I could not concentrate at all; my mind had literally shut down. Depression challenges God's original intention for our minds to be centers of activity.

Depression transforms activity into passivity. When passivity sets in, we become incapable of pushing out dark, irrational thoughts. In turn, such negativity leads to habitual, distorted thought patterns which reinforce our despair.

The writer of the Psalms sheds light on this: "You have put away my acquaintances far from me; You have made me an abomination to them; *I am* shut up, and cannot get out" (Psalm 88:8 NKJV). Reading the Bible became very difficult at the height of my depressive episodes, as passive shutdown blocked me from grasping the meaning of the Scriptures.

Loved ones and friends who do not understand the passivity of depression often inflicts additional injury to sufferers. It is extremely difficult for depressed individuals to accept advice. Therefore, family and friends must learn to actively listen to a depressed person.

In order to hear, we must listen with our eyes because 80 percent of communication is non-verbal; our hearts sense the emotions behind the words. Depressed individuals need to be befriended, rather than scolded or shamed.

Defense mechanisms, tainted by distorted thinking processes, construct walls of fear and shame within the minds of depressed individuals. Thought patterns determine whether individuals are able to interpret messages as blessings or curses.

In his book, *Ancient Paths,* Craig Hill, founder of Family Foundations International, amplifies this message:

> God intended that each person He created be permeated with a sense of His Glory. Glory can be defined as a feeling of dignity, great value of being, acceptability and legitimacy. Blessing of identity imparts God's Glory. On the other hand, cursing of identity delivers the opposite of Glory—Shame. Shame can be defined as a feeling of lack of dignity, worthlessness of being, unacceptability, and illegitimacy. God's purpose in life is to impart to you Glory through blessing. Satan's purpose is to Shame you through cursing.[18]

According to Hill, our thought processes follow one of two paths: God's glory or Satan's shame:

> Shame is a deep, deep wound of being that is a result of the cursing through identity. Shame, as opposed to guilt, is a deep feeling of wrongness of *BEING.* Guilt on the other hand, is a feeling of wrongness of *ACTION.* Guilt says, "I *MADE* a mistake." Shame says, "*I AM* a mistake." When shame is working, you feel like you have to work twice as hard as others to

---

18   Craig S. Hill, *The Ancient Paths* (Littleton, CO: Family Foundations, 1992), 78–79.

accomplish half as much. When you look at your peers, you feel like the only caterpillar in a butterfly world.[19]

Amidst the agony of depression, I began to wonder how my shame could be replaced by God's glory. Early one morning, while reading Ezekiel 47:1–12, my attention was turned to water, one of the metaphors of the Holy Spirit.

The Scripture passage talks about waters which heal—rising to cover one's ankles, knees, and waist before becoming deep enough to necessitate swimming. I began to picture the water flowing through my thought process. Wherever the water flows, it heals and brings life.

Like the healing flow of righteous waters, God wants to wash away our negative thoughts. Given the opportunity, the rivers of living water can wash away shame and negativity.

As my passivity began to dissipate, the freedom to grasp, acknowledge, and challenge thoughts slowly returned. Inspired by what God taught me in Ezekiel 47, I trudged forward.

Cursed by negativity, I needed a way to restructure my thought processes. The Apostle Paul's teaching in 2 Corinthians was my starting place. Paul talks about this problem as well as the strategic solution to break through strongholds that hold us hostage:

> "For the weapons of our warfare are not carnal but mighty in God for pulling down strongholds, casting down arguments and every high thing that exalts itself against the knowledge of God, bringing every thought into captivity to the obedience of Christ." (2 Corinthians 10:4–5 NKJV).

As I studied the phrase "bringing every thought into captivity,"

---

19   Ibid., 79.

I discovered it carries the idea of bringing my own negative emotions and destructive impulses into captivity. It gave me hope that God could eventually restructure my thought processes.

When the formula of thought—emotion, impulse, behavior—starts to form a foundation, it becomes imperative to understand the *time line* relationship between new thinking patterns and the emotions that follow. As determined as I was to try and think differently—more positively—I found it took time to retrain my thought processes.

God's Word always comes to us in seed form as evidenced by the parable of the sower. However, it takes time for seeds to germinate. With the passage of time, I discovered it would take approximately three weeks for my new thought processes to begin producing new emotions.

To believe *this* can happen, when we do not initially feel it, takes faith in action. The Holy Spirit taught me to ACT:

> **A***cceptance* of my current state-of-mind;
>
> **C***hoose* to think differently; and
>
> **T***rust* God by *faith* to restore my thought processes.

I want to share two examples of negative thinking patterns and how I used the above prescription to work through them.

As previously discussed in Chapter 1, my depression was linked to an irrational fear of knives. During my initial bout of depression, one particular knife frightened me. Most every time I saw it, I envisioned the blade coming after me.

Unfortunately, my wife used that knife to cut food regularly—I feared telling her about my fears would only make matters worse. The stronghold stayed in place for nine years, silently tormenting me on a daily basis.

During my second bout of depression, I shared the knife issue with my psychiatrist. He assured me for some people suffering with my condition it was common to be afraid of sharp objects. While such feedback was comforting, it did nothing to budge the negative stronghold.

Every time I saw the knife, panic exploded inside of me! As my depression began to dissipate, so did my passivity. Eventually, I was once again able to hear the Holy Spirit's still small voice in my thought process.

It was at that point He began to teach me to ACT to tear down these negative thinking patterns. The following is an analysis of how the knife stronghold was torn down using the ACT formula:

1. *Acceptance of my current state-of-mind.* It is one thing for us to acknowledge something, but accepting it as reality is an entirely different matter. To accept this dark onslaught of negative thinking was terribly frightening. My efforts to stop it only intensified my obsession.
    The Holy Spirit began to reveal my refusal to accept it was blocking the healing process. Dark thoughts remain fixed in place as long as they are insulated by darkness. Once exposed to the light, the horrible obsessions have no place left to hide. Embracing acceptance and allowing God's light to shine, my knife obsession began to lose its power. At this point, I was ready to move to the next step.

2. *Choose to think differently.* While it sounds simple, it takes real courage. Courage is resistance and mastery of fear, not the absence of fear. The only way I was going to

lose my fear of the knife was to tell myself the *truth* about it.

The truth concerning the knife: it is a kitchen utensil made to assist in preparing meals. It is not a destructive weapon that was going to magically leave the drawer, float through the air, and inflict harm on me or others. Having a new thought process in place, I was ready to move to the last step.

3. *Trust God by faith to restore my thought process.* The Bible says faith means the substance of things hoped for, and the evidence of things not seen. As mentioned, it took three to four weeks to modify my new thought processes. My faith, now clothed in courage, was ready to go the distance in order to transform negative thought patterns into positive ones, and, subsequently, alter my emotional outlook.

Today, that same knife is still housed in our kitchen. Every time I see it I am reminded God strengthened my faith through it.

A second example of my distorted, negative thinking involved television shows depicting violence. Whether it was the local news, cop shows, or movies, I eventually came to a place where I could barely watch television.

With my defense mechanisms drowned in a pool of passivity, irrational thoughts tortured me. Whether it was assuming the role of the victim or the evil perpetrator, I was paralyzed with fear. Consequently, I either turned the television off or left the room.

Using the ACT prescription, I was able to tear down the stronghold:

1. *Acceptance of my current state-of-mind.* By the grace of God, I was able to expose my dark, irrational fears of assuming the role of the victim or aggressor to the light of truth. Embracing the acceptance my sin nature was capable of thinking such things I was ready to move to the next step.

2. *Choose to think differently.* The only way I was going to lose my fear of watching violence on television was to tell myself the truth about it. The local news stories about violent acts were factual, but had no real connection to me. The violent television shows were mere fiction. In neither case was I the victim or aggressor. Having new thought processes in place, I was ready to move to the final step.

3. *Trust God by faith to restore my thought process.* Cloaking my faith with rationality and courage, I was able to confront my depression-induced fears. Today, I can watch real or depicted violence on television, yet separate myself from those stories.

As my negative thought patterns (strongholds) were torn down, one-by-one, my mind slowly moved away from the passivity that had imprisoned it. Rational thoughts yielded realistic, yet balanced emotions. It was a calm, spiritually-based breath of fresh air.

Paul prays specifically for all believers in Ephesians 3:16 and 19. He asks God to strengthen us by His Spirit, not with a brute strength, but a glorious inner strength. He further states God accomplishes this, not by pushing us around, but by His Spirit working deeply and gently within our hearts and minds.

As our inner person begins to quiet, God strengthens us with fresh courage, conquering our fear and despair. By constructing new thought processes, I achieved a state of emotional honesty, and was able to overcome the second major underlying factor contributing to my depression.

Chapter 8

Caution: Potential Destruction Ahead!

UNHEALTHY ANGER

Equipped with the ability to understand my losses and renew my thinking processes, a solid foundation was in place to examine the role anger played in the formation and perpetuation of my depressions. Anger manifests itself differently according to each individual.

Anger's landscape runs the gamut from highly explosive to total denial. The ultimate manifestations of extreme anger are homicide—anger turned outwards—and suicide—anger turned inwards. Other manifestations demonstrate total denial of anger, repressing the emotion from consciousness.

Genesis 1:27 introduces the thought human beings are made in the image of God, with various Scriptures citing numerous examples of His anger. The Hebrew word for anger appears approximately 455 times in the Old Testament, and on 375 separate occasions, specifically refers to the anger of God.[20]

---

20   Dwight L. Carlson, *Overcoming Hurts and Anger* (Eugene, OR: Harvest House, 1981), 38.

Many Christians have been taught anger is wrong, regardless of the circumstances. Sadly, we have been misled; we need look no further than to Jesus and His anger:

> Jesus became quite angry at times, contrary to the image we have of Him as a nice, quiet soul. When Jesus was about to heal the man with the paralyzed hand, He got upset at the hardened, calloused hearts of the onlookers around Him. The Bible says He looked "around at them with anger" (Mark 3:5). In Mark 11:15–17, we find Jesus driving out the parasitic money changers in the temple with a whip, shouting after them, "Is it not written, "My house shall be called a house of prayer for all nations? But you have made it robbers' den." In Matthew 23, He lashes out at the hypocritical Pharisees, calling them "white washed tombs...full of dead men's bones"! (v. 27).[21]

To further understand my anger, I began with a basic question: how did I get here? My clerical studies allowed me to realize I fit the "anger turned inward" category. The mystery was how and when did I choose to be an *anger in* person?

Dwight Carlson, Christian psychiatrist, offers insight:

> Anger is defined as an unpleasant emotional state of varying intensity from mild irritation to rage. It is a feeling of displeasure as a result of a real or imagined threat, insult, put-down, frustration, or injustice to you or to others who are important to you.[22]

After closely analyzing the definition, two particular phrases caught my attention: "unpleasant emotional state" and "feeling of

---

21   Ibid., 38–39.

22   Ibid., 49.

displeasure." My childhood temperament eliminated any desire for taking part in an unpleasant emotional state that caused feelings of displeasure because I did not like the way anger felt. It was quite easy to convince myself all anger was wrong. As the middle of five children, embracing the role of peacemaker made for safe camouflage.

Years before experiencing depression, people complimented my even-keel temperament. Many admired the fact I never seemed to get angry, which ultimately reinforced my *anger in* perception.

In my early twenties, my distorted perception developed into a belief: never getting angry was the equivalent of spiritual maturity. I remember telling my wife early in our marriage, as she grew in her faith, her outward anger tendencies would dissipate.

Sadly and pathetically, I sincerely embraced my own wisdom. In my mid-thirties, recovering from my second bout of depression, I started to accept the reality anger could be a contributory factor to my depression.

One common thread in describing anger is the concept of overstepping another person's boundaries. Bearing in mind we all like our space, Tim LaHaye, bestselling author of the *Left Behind* series, and Bob Phillips, family counselor, emphasize the idea of "territorial space":

> All human beings exercise what we call territorial space. Dad's favorite chair, my room, placing my coat or purse on a chair to save a seat at church or at a meeting—these are all indications that we want to protect what we think is "our territory." When territorial space is invaded, I have a tendency to become angry. If someone reads the paper over my shoulder, it bothers

me. If a man stands too close to my wife, I become upset. If someone fishes in my favorite fishing hole, I feel irritated. If a fellow employee crosses over into my job area and does some work, I feel threatened and uptight. If someone stares too long at me, I become provoked and think that it is none of their business. When territorial space is perceived as invaded, we all tend to become angry.[23]

Territorial space is a huge factor in activating our anger. Anger is a physiological response that occurs when someone or something oversteps our real or perceived boundaries.[24]

People with outward anger problems eventually explode when this physiological and emotional energy activates, particularly if others do not respond favorably to their demands. Those who turn their anger inward, mistakenly think this negative energy will simply go away.

Neil Clark Warren, psychologist and founder of E-harmony. com, uses the word "somatizer" to describe this (**Soma** is the Greek word for *body,* while **tizer** means *absorb*).[25] When I realized my body was acting as shock absorber for this energetic force I was adamantly denying, it was a profound wake up call.

My high blood pressure, colon problems, and skin rashes that the best doctors could not explain, were likely fueled by my anger. Researchers have long recognized that anger and other negative emotions are clearly linked with physical illnesses.

---

23 Tim LaHaye and Bob Phillips, *Anger Is a Choice* (Grand Rapids, MI: Zondervan, 2002), 32.

24 Neil Clark Warren, *Make Anger Your Ally* (Wheaton IL: Tyndale House Publishers, 1999).

25 Ibid.

Obviously, I needed to learn how to manage my anger, which undercut my old belief system. I thought the only ones who needed help were *anger out* people; the screamers and exploders! How wrong I was! Anger turned inward can be as destructive as outward manifestations of rage.

I once counseled a woman whose daughter frequently destroyed doors by hitting and slamming them. When I suggested she had as many anger issues as her daughter, she was dumbfounded.

As I pointed out the fruits of her anger—severe depression, suicide attempts, and life-threatening anorexia—a light passed over her countenance. For the first time, she became aware her inwardly-directed anger was causing as much or more destruction than her daughter's explosive outbursts. Individuals who do not acknowledge their anger often become depressed. Simply put, repressed anger fuels depression.

Learning to balance passivity and aggression is a major breakthrough in overcoming depression. The story of the lion and the owl offers a valuable lesson:

> The story is told of a ferocious lion that lived near a village next to the jungle. He developed the reputation of biting anyone who ventured into the jungle. When he was not biting people, he was chasing them as they ran for their lives. All the villagers were deathly afraid of the lion. One day, the villagers got together to discuss the problem of the ferocious lion. They all agreed to seek counsel and advice from the wise old owl. The villagers shared their fears with the wise old owl. He listened to all their concerns. Finally he said, "I think I know what to do. I'll take care of the problem." The wise old owl went and

visited the lion. He proceeded to tell the lion that his behavior was not acceptable. He shouldn't run around chasing people and biting them. The wise old owl told him that if he continued to behave in this way, he would become very lonely and would have no friends. He told the lion that it was very mean and self-ish to act the way he was acting. The lion sincerely apologized and promised the wise old owl that he would change his ways. Soon word got around about the change in the lion's behav-ior. The villagers began to venture into the jungle. Often they would see the lion sunning himself or drinking some water at the river. It wasn't long before people began walking close to the lion. They were losing their fear of him. As time passed, the villagers began to make faces and call the lion names as they walked by. This name-calling led to teasing the lion. The teasing escalated to pulling his tail, throwing rocks at him, and poking him with sticks. Eventually, the villagers began to chase the lion and hurt him even more ruthlessly. One day the wise old owl came to visit the lion. He found him hiding in a cave. He could see that the lion was bruised and bleeding from the tormenting received at the hands of the villagers. The wise old owl said "what happened to you?" "Well," said the lion, they are now chasing me, throwing rocks at me, and poking me with sticks." "I told you not to chase or bite the villagers," said the wise old owl. "But I didn't tell you not to roar."[26]

When I share this illustration with others, nearly everyone has the same response, expecting a different outcome. Assuming the owl was going to tell the previously angry lion he deserved his

---

26   Tim LaHaye and Bob Phillips, *Anger Is a Choice* (Grand Rapids, MI: Zondervan, 2002), 114–115.

plight, the words "but I didn't tell you not to roar" catches them off guard. Since anger is a part of daily life, remembering the *roar* reminds us: balance is possible in managing anger.

God wants to help us diffuse unhealthy anger and create new, healthier outlets for this powerful emotion. LaHaye and Phillips remind us of the importance of not *ignoring* or *eliminating* anger, but *understanding* it and *learning* where it comes from.[27]

As an *anger in* individual, I have spent most of my life trying to ignore and eliminate it, contributing to a series of physical problems. At fifty-three years of age (denial is powerful), I have come to the conclusion it is impossible to ignore or eliminate anger. If we do not work through our anger, it will extract a terrible physical and mental toll.

Dwight Carlson's book, *Overcoming Hurts and Anger,* has become my personal, daily guide for managing anger. Carlson is a diligent Bible student and a specialist in internal medicine and psychiatry. In previous chapters (Loss and Thinking), I shared personal strategies on how I work through losses and change thinking patterns. On the subject of anger, I use his strategies in chapters seven and eight:

1. Recognize your feelings
2. Delay taking any action
3. Pray for guidance
4. Identify the true cause of your anger
5. Evaluate whether your anger is legitimate
6. Determine a course of action
7. Forgive and forget[28]

---

27   Ibid., 8.

28   Dwight L. Carlson, *Overcoming Hurts and Anger* (Eugene, OR: Harvest House, 1981), 73, 75, 79, 81, 82, 104.

Proverbs 20:5 (HCSB) reads: "Counsel in a man's heart is deep water, but a man of understanding draws it up." God is using Dr. Carlson's work to draw my anger to the surface where I can better understand it.

God teaches us to forgive those who hurt us. Hurt often leads to anger. If the Holy Spirit is welcome in our hearts, we receive the necessary strength to forgive, and spare ourselves from unhealthy, unnecessary anger.

Consider Ephesians 4:25–27, 32 (NKJV): "Therefore laying aside falsehood, speak truth, each one of you, with his neighbor, for we are members of one another. Be angry and yet do not sin; do not let the sun go down on your anger, and do not give the devil an opportunity . . . be kind to one another, tender hearted, forgiving each other, just as God in Christ has also forgiven you."[29] Learning to balance my anger on a daily basis enabled me to overcome the third major underlying factor contributing to depression.

---

29   Ibid., 107.

Chapter 9

The Tender House of Compassion

HUMAN COMPASSION

Whereas my anger was hidden for years, the final major underlying factor contributing to my depression was on display for everyone. If there is one word to describe me, it was compassion. Human compassion, by itself, is very *fragile*—limited in what it can accomplish.

Many depressed individuals are overly sympathetic. Thinking back, my distorted internal battle-cry was if I did not feel someone's pain, I was not truly being compassionate. As my depressive state deepened, this battle-cry turned into a broken-cry—loving people the wrong way was killing me.

Researching compassion, I had one question: was it possible to be compassionate and remain healthy? I learned several things.

First, human compassion manifests itself through empathy and sympathy. According to *Merriam-Webster's Collegiate Dictionary*, empathy means being sensitive to and vicariously experiencing another's pain. Sympathy is an affinity or relationship whereas whatever affects one person or thing similarly affects the other.

Having someone *tell* us *about* his or her pain versus *feeling* his or her pain are worlds apart! Simply put, it is the difference between emotional health and burnout which, in many cases, leads to depression.

Second, over-responsibility is at the heart of unhealthy compassion. Subconsciously, my attempts to rescue others turned me into a magnet for their problems. Unfortunately, there is a sense of glorified self-importance and power that comes with being over-responsible.

John Westfall, Presbyterian minister and author of *Coloring Outside the Lines*, challenged me theologically:

> Over-responsibility is as much a sin as irresponsibility. The message inherent in over-responsibility is "God is not able, therefore I must take action. God is not strong enough or smart enough or involved enough to make a difference, so it's up to me to make things happen." Our need to take matters into our own hands is ultimately rooted in our unwillingness to let God be God and to believe that He is able.[30]

Ouch! My mind went immediately to James 4:17 which explains when a person knows what is right, but acts otherwise, he or she commits a sin. At first, the possibility of this being a sin surprised me, but then, in time, convicted me.

Third, it is important for each of us to grasp the concept of compassionate boundaries—for ourselves and the people we seek to help. Respecting the boundaries of those we love helps us become more empathetic.

---

30   John Westfall, *Coloring Outside The Lines* (San Francisco: Harper, 1991), 52.

Dr. Henry Cloud and John Townsend, co-authors of the best-seller, *Boundaries,* succinctly explain this idea:

> Loving others' boundaries confronts our self-centeredness. When we love and respect the boundaries of others, we accomplish two things. First, we genuinely care for the person. The second advantage in loving others' boundaries is that it teaches us empathy. It shows us that we need to treat others as we would like to be treated: "the entire law is summed up in a single command: 'Love your neighbor as yourself'" (Galatians 5:14).[31]

Fourth, I realized healthy human compassion can only go so far. I wanted to experience God's infinite compassion. *Com* means together, while *passion* comes from the Latin word *passus,* meaning the capacity to suffer.

Having already suffered enormous emotional pain, coming together with Christ to learn the capacity to suffer, and do it the right way, sounded great. I learned when we allow the compassion of Jesus to touch others, the Word of God flows freely to enable healing.

God does not need mini-Messiahs to promote the message of compassion. When overly-responsible mortals carry someone else's pain, they leave the creature (human) realm and usurp the Creator's role.

Henri Nouwen, bestselling author, clarifies the virtue of compassion:

> What does it mean to live in a world with a truly compassionate

---

31   Henry Cloud and John Townsend, *Boundaries* (Grand Rapids, MI: Zondervan, 1992), 282.

heart, a heart that remains open to all people at all times? It is very important to realize that compassion is more than sympathy or empathy. When we are asked to listen to the pains of people and empathize with their suffering, we soon reach our limits. God's heart is greater, infinitely greater, than the human heart. It is that divine heart God wants to give to us so that we can love all people without burning out or becoming numb. The Holy Spirit of God is given to people so they can become participants in God's compassion and reach out to all people at all times with God's heart. [32]

Expressing compassion God's way is an art. Jesus is the supreme artist, instilling compassion in our hearts. His compassion, working through us, is what our brothers and sisters need.

.

---

32   Henri Nouwen, *Here and Now* (New York: Crossroads, 1994), 109–110.

Chapter 10

Pinpointing Our Allegiance

THE POWER OF THE GRANDSTAND

The first doctoral seminar I attended at Fuller Theological Seminary was entitled "The Personal Health of the Minister." Those two weeks filled me with profound insight.

One particular insight (concept) was completely new to me. It was entitled "The Grandstand, Playing to an Audience of One," which allowed me to begin connecting the relational dots in my personal life. As time passed, it became apparent God was deeply influencing my inner person.

While working with the three hundred individuals I mentioned in the Introduction of this book, God enabled me to formulate this concept into a teaching model.

My protocol with a depressed person begins with a session to hear his or her story. Building upon that, I teach the individual four sessions on the factors that are the basis of depression—the seeds of loss, distorted thinking patterns, anger, and compassion.

I then introduce "The Grandstand Concept." This exercise

has proven to be extremely helpful. For some individuals, the intensity of their depression begins to lessen once they process this information.

The *Merriam-Webster's Collegiate Dictionary* defines grandstand as a raised set of seats, usually roofed, for spectators at a race track or sporting event. It is located in the center of the stands, providing the best view, and protection from the elements.

The *verb* form of grandstand means to play or act so as to impress onlookers. Hailing from South Africa, Dr. Hart used the sport of rugby to illustrate his model. A Southerner at heart, I chose college football.

The equivalent of a grandstand in a football stadium would be box seats. The box towering above the fifty yard line would represent the best seats. Imagine you as a 20 year old cheerleader or football player in your favorite team's colors. It is Saturday afternoon, there are 80,000 people in the stands, and the excitement is electric!

When the ball is kicked off, the adrenaline rush is incredible. As the crowd roars, the desire to perform well is overwhelming and exhilarating. Simply put, you are playing to the powerful influence of those around you.

Every day in our spiritual, mental, emotional, and physical lives we experience a parallel performance. Deep in our subconscious, we play to our grandstand of people; spectators who have influenced our lives profoundly, some positively, and others negatively.

These may be people we esteem highly such as parents, spouses, children, siblings, friends, employers, co-workers, and given others. Many of these same people may have hurt and wounded us deeply.

In the realm of the subconscious, these people are seated on the fifty yard line of our hearts, unchallenged. The tragedy unfolding at midfield is the most delicate, intimate part of our being.

At this point in the presentation, some individuals have asked and contemplated the same question. What is wrong with having role models and positive influences (spouses, parents, children, siblings, etc.) on the fifty yard line of our hearts? My reply, which catches many by surprise, is everything.

Only God is worthy to sit at the most coveted place in our hearts. People who profess to be Christians must place Jesus at midfield to occupy that position. Allowing other humans this position, we create invisible havoc.

When the Holy Spirit is unseated, our Christian inner lives become mediocre at best. How do we correct this? The answer rests in Colossians 1:18, where Paul proclaims Jesus must have first place in our lives.

Drawing a football stadium—a rectangular bowl with a lined field and two goalposts—for most individuals is instructional. Residing in South Carolina, I named my hypothetical field: Death Valley, the nickname for Clemson University's Memorial Stadium.

Unfortunately, we create a subconscious death valley when we allow loved ones to sit in that most delicate part of who we are. The following three examples illustrate this premise.

The first example involves a pastor's wife from a large church in a prominent denomination. When I first encountered this individual, her depression was so severe she could hardly function. After five sessions, the intensity of her depression remained quite severe.

When I introduced The Grandstand concept, she immediately began to weep uncontrollably. This exercise struck an open nerve in her heart. The church where her husband served was steeped in historical tradition, but negatively influenced by the senior staff member, a cantankerous, closed-minded individual.

Possessing a creative spirit, the pastor's wife was intimidated and demoralized by this ruthless, insensitive older man, who she had allowed to sit at midfield in her subconscious. With her mental faculties depressively shut down, she was unaware of the emotional damage her anger and unforgiving spirit were causing.

Realigning her emotional priorities, she was able to come face-to-face with her bitter spirit, and chose to forgive this man. It was indeed a holy moment when she mentally took his hand and walked him out of the stadium.

The second example involves a man who was verbally abused by his wife for years. By the time he saw me he had been hospitalized twice, had seen numerous psychiatrists, had taken several antidepressant medications, and had received electric shock therapy.

After teaching him the grandstand model, his depression improved significantly over the next three weeks! His countenance miraculously brightened as he took his wife's hand and walked her off his fifty yard line.

Removing her from midfield, he was now free to allow the Holy Spirit to heal his inner person by dealing with his losses, releasing his anger, and developing new thinking patterns. Consequently, he was able to stand up to her, freeing himself from her abusive control, and has yet to relapse into depression.

The third example is of a young woman in her early twenties who was trapped in a dysfunctional, live-in relationship. Her boyfriend loved to party, and was miserably lazy. He made a habit of putting her down while constantly mooching off her.

Having been raised in a Christian home, she had, like so many of us, strayed away from her relationship with God. Having already lived with this unsavory partner for three years, a part of her felt obligated to stay.

Depression had fogged her thinking; she simply could not decide whether to stay or leave. When I showed her the grandstand, she was reminded of the timeless adage, and told me she could not see the forest for the trees.

Suddenly, her eyes were open, and she was able to remove her boyfriend from midfield, creating space to enable a fresher encounter with God. She worked through her losses, developed new thinking patterns, discovered hidden anger, and eventually developed the strength to end this unhealthy relationship. In time, she met a responsible young man with likeminded values, fell in love, and married a much healthier partner.

Because The Grandstand is applicable to all of us, I want to share a simple personal example that does not directly involve depression. As might be expected, my father and older brother were among the spectators in my grandstand. While they were white collar, I was blue collar.

Both of them were invariably clad in long sleeve white dress shirts, while I wore short sleeve dress shirts. After mentally escorting them out of my grandstand, I entertained the possibility of wearing long sleeve dress shirts.

Being a pastor, I had ample opportunities to experiment with changing my wardrobe. To my surprise, I felt good about wearing them.

As we work through our grandstand issues, it is important to keep four things in mind. First, our fifty yard line is the most intimate, delicate part of our being. Second, only God Himself (Father,

Son, and Spirit) should occupy this most-privileged space. Anyone, except Him, will create an imbalance in our relationships, creating an emotional death valley.

Third, when a parent exerts negative influences, there is a natural tendency to go in the opposite direction. Move him or her out of our grandstand and allow God to create a new, guilt-free beginning.

Fourth, remember awareness and maintenance of a spiritual grandstand requires practice. I was first introduced to the grandstand theory in 1998. Fourteen years later, I invariably catch myself allowing others to temporally occupy my grandstand.

When I become aware of this unhealthy relapse I simply remove them, ask Him to forgive my sin of omission, and allow His Spirit to refill the void in my inner person. Without pinpointing our allegiance, our inner person will miss the daily opportunity to experience true peace, and hear the quiet, all-encompassing voice of God.

Chapter 11

Inner Fitness

A MUST IN OUR GROWTH AS DISCIPLES

Eleven years ago, I shared a sermon idea with a fellow minister pertaining to Psalm 46:10. Six months later while in the throes of another severe depression, I was sitting in a hospital waiting room, attempting to console others when the same minister walked by and whispered in my ear. Even though I was entrenched in the abyss, what he whispered penetrated the darkness and touched my heart.

When I first started taking antidepressants, I wondered if the medication could keep my depression at bay. I have since learned, while medications balance my moods, alone they are not capable of quieting and healing my inner person.

Individuals need *something* beyond themselves to remove the entrenched residue of depression. Psalm 46:10 became that something for me; it is the foundation from which God continues to heal and rebuild my inner person.

The first part of Psalm 46:10 reads: "Be still and know that I am God." The Hebrew Imperative for the words *be still* is what my minister friend whispered to me that day. The imperative is saying *for all who array themselves against God to lay down their weapons and realize they can't win.*

At some point in our lives all of us need to lay down our weapons; take a long, loving look at God; and quietly accept the fact He is in control. This allows Him to begin the process of quieting our inner person, whispering His love into our innermost being.

Determined to be a daily recipient of this whispering love, I started to enter my quiet times with no agenda, absolutely motiveless. Focused on being still, I began to experience this whispering love. The Holy Spirit gradually used this spiritual discipline to teach me the importance of building an inner fitness.

For most of my life, I have been bombarded with the necessity of outward fitness. While it has its place in the health of our well-being, an inner fitness is the key to growing spiritually. God has taught me a simple principle—how can He trust me with outward responsibility in His Kingdom if an inner fitness is not being established.

He longs for all of us to experience this whispering love. It is the door to growth and intimacy with Him.

In John 15:15, Jesus specifically calls us His friends. At first, entertaining the idea Jesus wanted to be my friend was puzzling. With mountains of self-condemnation and self-hatred within me, it was hard to envision myself as a worthy friend. At the time I simply felt unworthy to ask Him to remove the negativity.

From a human standpoint, my dilemma intensified while pondering the question: would I ever allow someone to get close to me if I did not think the individual liked me to begin with? As I pondered whether or not God likes me, I had to admit I did not think He did.

Subconsciously, I believed it was impossible for Him to like someone with a sin nature. Falling prey to deceit, I had kept God at arm's length.

It was much easier to believe God loves me as opposed to God *likes* me. Having been raised in a Christian home, I was constantly reassured God loved me. So, it was natural to respond yes to the question: does God love me?

Numerous times, I have asked individuals: does God love you? As opposed to: does God like you?

Most say yes to the first, but invariably answer no to the second. I then follow-up with the very question that has long tormented me: how many people will we allow to get close to us, if we do not think they like us?

Not surprisingly, the answer was none. It was here where I was able to share my former erroneous belief and help others realize God likes them.

Christians often sing "What a Friend We Have in Jesus," yet fail to experience the true meaning of the hymn. A great privilege of mine has been to see God transform broken people to the point where they accept the reality Jesus is truly their best friend!

As we grow in our friendship with Jesus, we cannot help, but notice His humility. The closer I grow to Him, the clearer it becomes that humility (I would recommend reading Andrew Murray's book, *Humility*) was His chief virtue to which all other virtues flowed.

For us to truly understand humility, we must overcome the unconscious pride that invariably hides this golden virtue. Around the sixth century, the seven deadly sins (pride, envy, anger, sloth, greed, gluttony, and lust) were adopted by the Christian faith as the seven cancers, reinforcing the power of sin, and mangling our desires, pointing us toward poisonous delights.[33]

Of the seven sins, pride is the most deadly because it elevates the individual to a God-like status. It empowers us to dictate our futures and make our rules. Pride attaches and wraps itself around the other six sins, making them all the more potent. In American society, to our detriment, pride has been elevated to a virtue status by many.

Part of our hidden pride is avoiding pain; especially, when stigmata are attached. Often, depressed individuals are in denial about the severity of their condition. As depression intensifies, the individual is exposed to the horrific side of the sin nature, causing extreme shame.

The vast majority of depressed individuals feel like God has abandoned them. To entertain the thought God could be refining our inner person is difficult to comprehend. Only one power in the universe can supplant pride—humility.

The Scriptures tell us in order to be a disciple of Jesus, one must deny self-interest, take up his or her cross daily, and follow Him. Simply put, one must trust God for the power to abandon selfishness and allow the Spirit of Christ to fill the void.

Jesus modeled humility daily and His mission of salvation for mankind was wrapped in it. As Christian disciples, we must take hold of humility as our chief virtue. A transformational breakthrough occurs when we learn to view ourselves through the virtue of humility,

All of a sudden, life being all about us starts to fall by the wayside. It becomes a breath of fresh air to entertain the thought life is about Him and serving His creation.

---

33 Jeff Cook, *Seven* (Grand Rapids, MI: Zondervan), 14–15.

For those of us who have experienced depression, part of our mission in the kingdom of God could be to serve a brother or sister experiencing adversity. Proverbs 17:17 (NKJV) reads: "A friend loves at all times and a brother [or sister] is born for adversity." Someone who has walked the same broken road often makes for the best comforter.

Depressed individuals need encouragement. Without it, they fall prey to well-intentioned people with misguided messages. Proverbs 25:20 (NLT) warns against misguided messages: "Singing cheerful songs to a person whose heart is heavy is as bad as stealing someone's jacket in cold weather or rubbing salt in a wound."

For those who have not experienced depression, be careful with word choice and attitude when addressing a depressed loved one or friend. A light-hearted approach may indicate a flippant attitude, further alienating him or her.

During the first four years of my personal relationship with Jesus (before suffering depression), I experienced joy unspeakable. In retrospect, the depth of my discipleship, in spite of boundless enthusiasm, was shallow. Having suffered repeated bouts of depression, my discipleship is now broader and deeper.

I solemnly believe in the message conveyed by Psalm 1:3 and Jeremiah 17:8, describing a tree, planted by living waters, whose branches stay green and produce fruit, even in times of drought. The simple, but profound words contained in 2 Corinthians 4:7 (NLT) have germinated, and are rooted deeply within my heart:

But this precious treasure—this light and power that now shines within us—is held in perishable containers, that is, in our weak bodies. So everyone can see that our glorious power is from God and is not our own.

Consistently hearing from God has enabled me to embrace Jesus' friendship. Embracing Jesus' friendship has taught me I must choose humility to be my chief virtue.

Choosing the virtue of humility daily, His Spirit empowers me to befriend and comfort others. In all of this, He continues to build my inner fitness.

Part III

Dear Church:

Please Join Us, We Need You . . .

Chapter 12

Pastor Please

What a gift it would be for us to come together in the Christian community to help in the comforting process. A synergy that is holistic and creative can result from combining pastors' efforts with family members, physicians, counselors, and emotionally mission-minded people.

The mission of the church regarding emotional trauma can be furthered and fruitful. As a survivor of five clinical depressions, I would be gratified to see the church enter the arena of mental health, and through the leadership of the Holy Spirit and our friendship, become a vital part in the healing process.

As a former pastor of a local church, I understand the underlying dynamics pastors face. When 60 percent of a congregation does not understand the other 40 percent are struggling with emotional issues, it can be tough to convince the unaffected group there is a real need to establish frontline ministry.

I know there is friction between what pastors perceive their role to be versus that of his or her laity. Some pastors mistakenly believe

93

they are the only ones spiritually and emotionally equipped to help those in despair. Not surprisingly, many lay people think pastors should be the sole source of spiritual comfort.

In some churches, depression and anxiety are anathema—much the same as divorce was once viewed. Unfortunately, there are pockets in certain denominations, still treating divorced people like second class citizens even though 55 percent of the adult population experiences divorce.

In his book, *Preacher Behave,* J. Clark Hensley writes about the untouchables:

> Someone has said that the army of the Lord is the only one in which they shoot the wounded. The statement is made in reference to the treatment by pastors and church family people of alcoholics, divorcees and other people who are a part of the church's "leper colony'"—the untouchables. Dozens of times I've heard the lament from a divorced person: "I find that I do not have a Christian friend in my church, one who will come to me or one to whom I can go, who understands my needs. My pastor shuns me; my Sunday school teacher gives me little attention. At a time when I need someone so much, there seems to be no one to turn to." If these were isolated cases it would be bad enough. But they are very common. "Brethren, if a man be overtaken in a fault, ye which are spiritual restore such a one in a spirit of meekness, considering yourself lest ye also be tempted." Gal. 6:1. Maybe the key here is ye which are spiritual. It is unforgivable to neglect those in the leper colony. Jesus touched them. Surely the pastor can make himself available. What do you say to them? Why say anything? Except

"I'm praying for you." "I'm sorry." "I care." "I'm concerned."
"Is there anything I can do?" "I'm ready to listen— to cry with
you—to pray with you."[34]

Today, by the grace of God, increasingly more churches are
treating this group of untouchables with grace and dignity. Whereas
divorce and addiction have become the focus of some discipleship
programs in the church, depression and anxiety—for the most
part—have been left to the professional world. By befriending the
depressed, the church can actively extend its mission.

THE ROLE OF PASTORAL COUNSELING

Pastoral counseling has become a major player in mental health
treatment. Pastoral counseling is perhaps more diversified than professional counseling services. Christian groups like the American
Association of Christian Counselors (AACC) are professionally
licensed counselors with thousands of members throughout the
United States.

Conversely, pastors of local churches, particularly small to me-
dium-sized congregations, are less accountable to a specific code
of ethics. Moreover, a rigid theological stance may complicate the
definition of counseling.

For example, some pastors believe Bible study is the sole method
for dealing with troubled souls. Other pastors believe if the denomination is not involved in the counseling process, counselees have
gone adrift. Some pastors opt out of the process, claiming they are
not gifted for the task. They choose to refer their parishioners to
professional Christian therapists.

Some pastors are problem-focused, while others are solution-

---

34   J. Clark Hensley, *Preacher Behave!* (Jackson, MS: Dallas Printing Co., 1985), 62–63.

focused. Based on my personal experience, solution-focused pastoral counseling is often more effective than problem-focused modalities.

In his book, *Solution-Focused Pastoral Counseling*, Dr. Charles A. Kollar offers these ethical guidelines for pastors who counsel:

1. Be informed by a theoretical framework of identity formation and therapeutic assumptions.
2. The rights of the counselee are primary.
3. Make every effort to refrain from dual relationships. Remain alert to your limitations.
4. Counseling must be confidential.
5. Be sure the counselee is aware of the responsibilities or limitations of the counseling relationship.
6. The counselor must not become romantically or sexually intimate with a counselee.
7. Do not use diagnostic or treatment procedures that you have not been professionally trained in.[35]

Kollar's ethical guidelines are similar to those outlined for professional counselors. To some extent, his seven guidelines are covered in the regulations governing professional counselors.

While it is true pastors are more limited in their counseling roles, they are in a wonderful position to encourage their local churches to reach out to other parts of the body of Christ—Christian physicians and counselors. Solution-focused counseling encourages pastors to attempt resolution in two or three sessions. If the counseling proves to be insufficient, referrals can be made to Christian-oriented professional counselors who have the training and expertise to deal

---

35   Charles Allen Kollar, *Solution-Focused Pastoral Counseling* (Grand Rapids, MI: Zondervan, 1997), 96.

with the issues at hand.

My first-hand experience has taught me a pastor's calling is diverse and labor intensive—regular study, discipleship, visitations, baptism, and conduction of weddings and funerals. With such a varied and complex job description, many pastors do not have time to provide comprehensive pastoral counseling.

Therefore, I encourage pastors attempting to befriend the depressed to share the burden with strategic laypeople who are suited (2 Corinthians 1:3–4) for the task of dealing with the emotional problems of their congregations. Spiritually-gifted, experienced laypeople can lighten the load while assuming a major role in ministering to the depressed and anxious. Ultimately, pastors can empower the laity to become caregivers by actively encouraging them. Such preparation is integral to the compassionate efforts of the church in the twenty-first century.

GROUNDING THE CONCEPT OF MINISTRY IN THE LOCAL CHURCH

Befriending and comforting depressed persons can be grounded in the local church through the avenue of discipleship. Depressed people can benefit from addressing the following five areas:

1. Learn to integrate faith and pain,
2. Personally experience emotional healing,
3. Grow and mature as disciples,
4. Become equipped to communicate the gospel more meaningfully and effectively, and
5. Refine their life purpose.

Proverbs 13:20 tells us those who walk with the wise will grow wise. Those in congregations who commit themselves to helping depressed persons must be examples of health and emotional honesty. Through the power of the Holy Spirit, those befriending disciples can communicate authentically, create a spiritual community with those they are helping, and serve as vessels for God's compassion.

Many are aware of the cliché stating churches are hotels for saints, rather than hospitals for sinners. Befriending disciples can enable churches to become hospitals for saints and sinners. Churches can take the lead to provide educated, compassionate laypersons to befriend depressed individuals.

In his book, *The Purpose Driven Church,* Rick Warren, senior pastor of Saddleback Community Church, poses five questions concerning Christian education or discipleship programs:

1. Are people learning the content and meaning of the Bible?
2. Are people seeing themselves, life, and other people more clearly from God's perspective?
3. Are people's values becoming more aligned with God's values?
4. Are people becoming more skilled in serving God?
5. Are people becoming more like Christ?[36]

Growth in those five areas is critical to the overall health of the church. Befriending depressed individuals through Christ certainly encompasses the aforementioned categories.

STAGGERING NUMBERS

In 2008, 57.7 million Americans (18 and above) suffered from serious mental disorder (including major depression, bipolar disorder, schizophrenia, dysthymic disorder, and anxiety disorders at

---

36   Rick Warren, *The Purpose Driven Church* (Grand Rapids, MI: Zondervan, 1995), 362.

any given point in time).[37] The World Health Organization reports "mental illness in the United States and Canada is now the leading cause of disability for people ages 15-44."[38] Chapter 14 of this book serves as a quick reference guide highlighting different types of depression.

A PERSONAL INVITATION PASTOR

Where do people with disabilities fit into the Kingdom of God? Jesus spent two-thirds of His life ministering to the hurting and disabled. Ironically, many of today's churches do not attempt to minister to these same people. Regarding ministry extended to depressed and anxious persons, the percentage is sadly even lower.

Unfortunately, over thirty thousand people a year commit suicide in our nation. It is a cold hard fact—90 percent of these people have a mood disorder. Unfortunately, our priorities as a collective church are upside down. Every pastor is encouraged to stand in the gap to turn this state of affairs right side up for the glory of God!

---

37   National Institute of Mental Health, *The Numbers Count: Mental Disorders in America* (Bethesda, MD: NIH Publication # 01-4584, 2007), 1.

38   Ibid.

Chapter 13

Dying on the Emotional Battlefield

FROM MY HEART TO YOURS

I want to make a personal appeal to those individuals contemplating suicide. Having been where you currently are, please listen.

First and foremost, suicide is always a permanent solution to a temporary problem. If you are standing at this horrible threshold, what brought you here? Are you so angry at God and those who have hurt you, you want to hurt them back? Do you honestly think your family and friends would be better off without you? Both ideas are rooted in destructive anger and extreme selfishness.

Instead of giving in to strong internal impulses screaming for you to commit suicide, resist the urge! Exodus 34:7 explains our sins go to the third and fourth generations. Simply put, all of your family members, including extended family—aunts, uncles, cousins, etc.—will be affected by your selfish act for three to four generations.

From the depths of my heart, I beg you not to take your life. Instead, seek help. God gave you life, and it is His right to take it when He chooses. If God can sustain me through five severe bouts of depression laced with suicidal thinking, He is more than able to pull you through your current crisis. God wants to help you; please let Him.

For families that have lost a loved one to suicide, I pray you will allow God's mercy to bathe and comfort your hearts. I encourage you to read the suicide contagion section in this chapter to possibly head off another tragedy.

Some people struggle, wondering where their loved one will spend eternity. Remember, he or she is in the hands of a *holy, righteous, merciful* God. His ways are not our ways, and His thoughts are not our thoughts. Only He truly knows our loved one's hearts—leave that part up to Him.

Join me in befriending the depressed. The following is helpful and sobering information about suicide.

SUICIDE FACTS

Suicide is a frightful and tragic consequence of some 15 percent of depressions. Research shows most people who kill themselves often have a diagnosable mental disorder or substance abuse issue, or both. The majority have a depressive illness.

Suicide is a complex behavior usually caused by a combination of factors. Studies indicate the most promising way to prevent suicidal behavior is through early recognition, intervention, and treatment of depression and other psychiatric illnesses.

Most depressed people—approximately 85 percent—do not kill themselves. Still, the probability 15 percent of the depressed population may take their own lives, soberly reinforces the fact depression is a deadly disease. Any concerns about suicidal risk should always be taken seriously and immediately evaluated by a qualified professional.

WARNING SIGNS

1. Changes in behavior, including eating/sleeping patterns
2. Threat, casual mention, or fear of suicide
3. Feelings of hopelessness/worthlessness
4. Giving away prized possessions; setting final arrangements
5. Previous suicide attempts[39]

RISK FACTORS

The following are among the risk factors leading to suicide:

1. One or more diagnosable mental or substance abuse disorders
2. Impulsivity
3. Adverse life events
4. Family history of mental or substance abuse disorder
5. Family history of suicide
6. Family violence, including physical or sexual abuse
7. Prior suicide attempt
8. Firearm in the home
9. Incarceration

---

39   Nicole Elizabeth Southgate, "Suicide Prevention" (speech, Rotary Club meeting, Greer, SC, March 2004).

10. Exposure to the suicidal behavior of others, including family, peers, or in the news or fiction stories[40]

COST TO THE NATION

1. Suicide takes the lives of more than 30,000 Americans every year.

2. Every 18 minutes, someone in the United States commits suicide.

3. Every day, 80 Americans take their lives and over 1,900 Americans visit emergency departments for self-inflicted injury (National Hospital Ambulatory Medical Care Survey, total 706,000).

4. Suicide is now the 11th leading cause of death in the United States.

5. For every two victims of homicide in the U.S. there are three persons who commit suicide.

6. There are now twice as many deaths due to suicide than from AIDS.

7. Between 1952 and 1995, the incidence of suicide among adolescents and young adults nearly tripled.

8. In the month prior to their suicide, 75 percent of elderly persons visit a physician.

9. Over half of all suicides occur in adult men, age 25–65.

40　National Institute of Mental Health, *Suicide Facts*, NIMH Publication, 1999, cited by Mental Health Matters http://www.mental-health-matters.com/articles/article.php?artID=390 (accessed March 27, 2006; page now discontinued), 1.

10. Many who attempt suicide never seek professional care.

11. Males are 3 to 4 times more likely than females to die from suicide because they employ more lethal means (firearms, hanging etc.).

12. More teenagers and young adults die from suicide than from cancer, heart disease, AIDS, birth defects, stroke, pneumonia, and influenza, and chronic lung disease, combined.[41]

Suicide Contagion

Suicide contagion refers to exposure to suicide or suicidal behaviors within one's family or peer group, or through media reports of suicide. All of which can result in an increase in suicide attempts. Direct and indirect exposure to suicidal behavior has been shown to increase the risk for suicide attempts, particularly among adolescents and young adults.

The risk for suicide contagion is often magnified by a sensationalist media because suicide is the result of many complex factors. The media should not attempt to provide oversimplified explanations for a tragedy such as recent negative life events or acute stressors.

Media reports should not indulge in detailed descriptions of the method of suicide to avoid copycat behaviors. News reports should not glorify the victim nor imply suicide was effective in calling attention to the victim's sense of despair. Instead, information about suicide hotlines or emergency contacts should be provided to those at risk for suicide.

---

41   National Strategy for Suicide Prevention, *Suicide: Cost to the Nation*, http://www. mentalhealth.samhsa.gov/suicideprevention/costtonation.asp, 1 (accessed March 27, 2006; page now discontinued).

Following exposure to suicide or suicidal behaviors within one's family or peer group, individuals at risk for adopting those same acts should be evaluated by a mental health professional. Persons deemed at risk for suicide should undergo a thorough mental health evaluation.

HELP AND PREVENTION

It is a myth that talking about suicide either maximizes or minimizes the risk of self-harm behaviors. Those at risk for suicide often discuss their deaths prior to killing themselves. People in crisis may be unwilling to seek help on their own. Depressed individuals need to be reminded effective treatment for depression is available.

PREVENTION PROGRAMS

Studies have shown successful suicide prevention programs readily identify serious psychiatric illnesses, and help those in despair to improve their coping skills, control aggression, and provide appropriate medical therapy. All suicide prevention programs should be subjected to rigorous standards to measure efficacy and safety.

A FINAL NOTE

In the epilogue of her book, *Night Falls Fast*, psychologist, Kay Redfield Jamison, writes:

> Like many of my colleagues who study suicide, I have seen time and again the limitations of our science, been privileged to see how good some doctors are and appalled by the callousness and incompetence of others. Mostly I have been *impressed* by how **little value our society** puts on saving the lives of those who are in such despair as to want to end them. It is a societal illusion that suicide is rare. It is not. Certainly the mental illnesses most closely tied to suicide are not rare. They

are common conditions, and unlike cancer and heart disease, they disproportionately affect and kill the young.[42] (bold added, emphasis mine)

Jamison's quote is a wake-up for all Christians to seriously acknowledge the harsh reality of suicide. It is also an admonition for the church to assist with suicide prevention.

---

42   Kay Redford Jamison, *Night Falls Fast* (New York: Vintage Books, 1999), 310.

Chapter 14

Quick Reference Guide:

THE DIFFERENT FORMS OF DEPRESSION

NORMAL SADNESS VS. DEPRESSION

People experience sadness from time to time, and feelings of depression are certainly part of that experience. It is not normal, however, if an individual becomes unusually sad and begins to lose interest in pleasurable activities without reason.

Clinical depression is not some passing blue mood or a sign of personal weakness. It cannot be merely wished away—depression can last for months or years. If left untreated, results can range from disrupted relationships to loss of professional productivity to disability to death.

The *Textbook of Psychiatry* describes the general characteristics of depression:

> Depression is a term with meanings ranging from transient
> dips in mood that are characteristic of life itself, to a clinical
> syndrome of substantial severity, duration, and associated signs
> and symptoms that is markedly different from normal. Grief,
> or bereavement, encompasses features of a depressive syndrome
> but is usually less pervasive and more limited in duration.

The clinical features of depression fall into four broad categories:

1. **Mood (affect):** sad, blue, depressed, unhappy, down-in-the-dumps, empty, worried, irritable.

2. **Cognition:** loss of interest, difficulty concentrating, low self esteem, negative thoughts, indecisiveness, guilt, suicidal ideation, hallucinations, delusions.

3. **Behavior:** psychomotor retardation or agitation, crying, social withdrawal, dependency, suicide.

4. **Somatic (physical):** sleep disturbance (insomnia or hypersomnia), fatigue, decreased or increased appetite, weight loss or gain, pain, gastrointestinal upset, decreased libido.[43]

DIFFERENT FORMS OF DEPRESSION

Depression wears multiple, complicated faces. It confuses those trying to make sense out of it. Depression can be divided into two broad categories: situational and biological.

SITUATIONAL DEPRESSION

Situational depression results from reaction to losses that directly alter an individual's thought patterns, as well transiently affecting sleep, energy, appetite, and enthusiasm. Most people experience one or more situational depressions at some point during their lives.

Situational depression does not typically require medication, but psychotherapy and counseling may be helpful. In some cases, situational lows can evolve into biological depression, particularly if the losses are neglected and internal conflicts remain unresolved.

---

43   Robert E. Hales, Stuart C. Yudofsky, and John A. Talbott. *Textbook of Psychiatry, 2nd ed.* (Washington, D.C.: American Psychiatric Press, 1994), 467.

BIOLOGICAL DEPRESSION

Biological depression—also known as major depressive episodes—results from chemical imbalance. A combination of medication and counseling/therapy are essential to recovery.

Many depressed people describe a dark cloud hanging over their heads. An individual experiencing the dark cloud for a portion of the day may well be suffering from situational depression. However, with biological depression, the dark cloud is a dominant feature present throughout the day, although the person may feel increasingly depressed at certain times of the day, particularly early in the morning.

DYSTHYMIC DISORDER

Dysthymia is a mild, but chronic, form of depression. Dysthymia (dis-THI-me-uh) symptoms usually last for at least two years, and often for much longer. Although dysthymia symptoms may be less intense than those of depression, dysthymia can actually affect your life more seriously because it lasts for so long. With dysthymia, you may lose interest in normal daily activities, feel hopeless, lack productivity and have a low self-esteem. People with dysthymia are often thought of as being overly critical, constantly complaining and incapable of having fun.[44]

SEASONAL AFFECTIVE DISORDER

Seasonal affective disorder (also called SAD) is a type of depression that occurs at the same time every year. If you are like most people with seasonal affective disorder, your symptoms start in the fall and may continue into the winter months, sapping your

---

44   Mayo Clinic Staff, "Dysthymia." Mayo Foundation for Medical Education and Research, http://www.mayoclinic.com/health/dysthymia/DS01111 (access [December 20, 2012])

energy and making you feel moody. Less often, seasonal affective disorder causes depression in the spring or early summer. Treatment for seasonal affective disorder includes light therapy (phototherapy), psychotherapy and medications. Don't brush off that yearly feeling as simply a case of the "winter blues" or a seasonal funk that you have to tough out on your own. Take steps to keep your mood and motivation steady throughout the year.[45]

BIPOLAR I DISORDER

The term bipolar disorder is synonymous with manic-depressive disorder. By definition, bipolar means two opposite poles, mania on the one end, and depression on the other. The criteria for a manic episode as defined by the American Psychiatric Association's Diagnostic and Statistical Manual of Mental Disorders, Fourth Edition (DSM IV) are as follows:

A. A distinct period of abnormality and persistently elevated, expansive, or irritable mood, lasting at least one week (or any duration if hospitalization is necessary).

B. During the period of mood disturbance, three (or more) of the following symptoms have persisted (four if the mood is only irritable) and have been present to a significant degree:

(1) inflated self-esteem or grandiosity

(2) decreased need for sleep (e.g., feels rested after only three hours of sleep)

(3) more talkative than usual or pressure to keep talking

---

45   Mayo Clinic Staff, "Seasonal affective disorder (SAD)." Mayo Foundation for Medical Education and Research, http://www.mayoclinic.com/health/seasonal-affective-disorder/DS00195 (access [September 22, 2011]).

(4) flight of ideas or subjective experience that thoughts are racing

(5) distractibility (i.e., attention too easily drawn to unimportant or irrelevant external stimuli)

(6) increase in goal-directed activity (either socially, at work or school, or sexually) or psychomotor agitation

(7) excessive involvement in pleasurable activities that have a high potential for painful consequences (e.g., engaging in unrestrained buying sprees, sexual indiscretions, or foolish business investments).[46]

BIPOLAR II DISORDER

The main difference between Bipolar I and II disorder is in the latter, the magnitude of the elevated mood is less intense. The individual suffering from Bipolar II disorder experiences full-fledged major depressive episodes, but instead of manic episodes, he or she experiences hypomanic episodes—abnormally elevated moods not as intense as full-blown mania. In other words, the decreased need for sleep, racing thoughts, grandiosity, impulsiveness, agitation/euphoria, etc. are less intense—hence the name *hypo*mania.

The criteria for Bipolar II are as follows:

A. Presence (or history) of one or more Major Depressive Episodes

B. Presence (or history) of at least one Hypomanic Episode

C. There has never been a Manic Episode or Mixed Episode—mixed means simultaneous manic and

---

46 American Psychiatric Association, *Diagnostic and Statistical Manual of Mental Disorders*, 4th ed. (Washington, D.C.: American Psychiatric Association, 1994), 332.

depressive symptoms such as someone who is tearful, and dysphoric while experiencing racing thoughts and excessive energy at the same time

D. The mood symptoms in Criteria A and B are not better accounted for by Schizoaffective Disorder and are not superimposed on Schizophrenia, Schizophreniform Disorder, Delusional Disorder, or Psychotic Disorder Not Otherwise Specified.

E. The symptoms cause clinically significant distress or impairment in social, occupational, or other important areas of functioning.[47]

CYCLOTHYMIC DISORDER

Cyclothymia (si-klo-THIGH-me-uh), also called cyclothymic disorder, is a mood disorder. Cyclothymia causes emotional ups and downs, but they are not as extreme as in Bipolar I and II mood cycles.

With cyclothymia, a person experiences periods when his or her mood noticeably shifts up and down from his or her baseline. The individual may feel on top of the world for a time, followed by a low period when he or she feels somewhat blue. Between these cyclothymic highs and lows, a person may feel stable and fine.

Compared with Bipolar I and II, the highs and lows of cyclothymia are less extreme. Still it is critical to seek help to manage these symptoms because they increase a person's risk of Bipolar I and II.

When a person has cyclothymia, he or she can typically function in daily life, though not always well. The unpredictable nature

---

47 American Psychiatric Association, *Diagnostic and Statistical Manual of Mental Disorders*, 4th ed. (Washington, D.C.: American Psychiatric Association, 2000), 397.

of the person's mood shifts may significantly disrupt his or her life because you never know how you are going to feel.[48]

POSTPARTUM DEPRESSION

Biologically-based, postpartum depression is non-discriminatory, affecting many women during what should be the happiest time of their life cycle—birth of a child. The MGH Center for Women's Mental Health reports:

> During the postpartum period, about 85% of women experience some type of mood disturbance. Most experience *the postpartum blues*; the symptoms are mild and short lived. Rather than feelings of sadness, women with the blues more commonly report mood lability, tearfulness, anxiety or irritability. These symptoms usually peak on the fourth or fifth day after delivery and may last for a few hours or a few days, remitting spontaneously within two weeks of delivery. *Postpartum depression* affects 10% to 15% of women. Whereas the postpartum blues need no treatment, postpartum depression is serious and needs to be treated just like major depression. Postpartum psychosis is the most serious postpartum condition, affecting 1.5% of women. Those individuals loss touch with reality. [49]

SITUATIONAL AND BIOLOGICAL DEPRESSIONS ARE TREATABLE

Situational and biological depressions are treatable and about 85

---

48   Mayo Clinic Staff, "Cyclothymia." Mayo Foundation for Medical Education and Research, http://www.mayoclinic.com/health/cyclothymia/DS00729 (access [June 13, 2012]).

49   MGH Center for Women's Mental Health, *Postpartum Psychiatric Disorders*, 2008. http://www.womensmentalhealth.org/library/postpartum-psychiatric-disorders/

percent of patients respond to treatment by the end of one year.[50] Unfortunately, half of the people who suffer from depression do not seek treatment.

One out of every sixteen adults experience biological depression at some point in their lives. Women are twice as likely as men to suffer from severe depression. Possible reasons women are two times more likely than men to be depressed are genetics and hormonal influences, both of which might make them more vulnerable.

Societal stigma plays a big role—men underreport depression because it is not deemed masculine. The prevalence of depression places it among the most frequent and debilitating of all illnesses.

Silent Epidemic

Depression has been described as a silent epidemic. Undoubtedly, depressed individuals withdraw and hide, as described by Christian author David Hazard, in his book, *Breaking Free from Depression*:

> Keep in mind that depression can become hidden if we have a natural tendency to minimize our problems and symptoms. This is often the case with very capable people. We mask our problems with a façade of "can-do" determination. We get by in life telling ourselves, "What I'm feeling is no big deal. I can handle this." For some of us that's a fact. We can handle a lot. But when we think this way, we condition ourselves to accommodate way too many dark and dismal moods—until feeling down seems pretty normal. By then we've lost sight of the fact that we are depressed![51]

50   Jeffery K. Smith, "Mood Disorders" (keynote address, winter board meeting of H.I.M. Ministries, Easley, SC, February 5, 2004).

51   David Hazard, *Breaking Free from Depression* (Eugene, OR: Harvest House, 2002),

Without the proper knowledge to understand what we are up against, this silent epidemic will continue. Even in the midst of great pain, and facing the reality it will not go away quickly, there is comfort in understanding the basis of depression.

Conclusion

A Personal Note

By the *mercy* of God, I have written this book as someone who has survived numerous bouts of depression. Since my depression is a chronic, recurrent illness, it is necessary for me to take prescribed maintenance medications. I consider the medication as a gift from God.

The healing Jesus has brought me through His Word is clearly evident. The caregivers God strategically placed in my path have immeasurably aided my recovery. The compatibility of my faith and available medical treatments for depression have truly freed me to live and love.

The powerful blow depression leaves on our souls—mind, emotions and will—causes a deeply embedded bruise and, depending on the severity, leaves us emotionally handicapped, to some degree. We live in a broken world full of hurting individuals who need someone to befriend them.

The truth is 16 percent of the general population will experience depression in their lifetime, while another 4 percent will experience bipolar disorder—a combined twenty out of every one hundred people. Adding in people who struggle with the many forms of anxiety disorders, the numbers are staggering.

Thank God we do not have to confront this burden alone. Moving by faith in God's infinite mercy, we trust His perfect timing to guide specific individuals who cross our paths. Equipped with insights on differentiating loss, changing negative thinking patterns, managing anger, practicing healthy compassion, and guarding our grandstand, we prepare to comfort others, as illustrated in 2 Corinthians 1:3–4.

BECOMING PART OF THE SOLUTION

I hope readers will use these shared insights about depression, allowing the Holy Spirit to guide each of you to help people experiencing emotional pain. The responsibility of nurturing depressed people need not rest solely in the hands of physicians, counselors, and therapists.

The goal is not to take the place of professionals, but to join them as caregivers in the healing process. Together, we can provide a healing atmosphere for depressed persons and, most importantly, allow Jesus to reveal His never-ending mercies, unconditional love, and holiness.

While the Holy Spirit inspires your empathetic mission, may God bless and protect you (Psalm 91). Even in the darkest of times, our pain will eventually come full circle and take us deeper into the heart of God.

Bathed in His mercy (Lamentations 3:22),
Greg L. Russ

Bibliography

American Leprosy Missions, *The Disease.* http://www.leprosy. org/LEPdisease.html (accessed March 27, 2006; page now discontinued).

———. *Leprosy Facts and Myths.* http://www.leprosy.org/ LEPinfo. html (accessed March 27, 2006; page now discontinued).

American Psychiatric Association. *Diagnostic and Statistical Manual of Mental Disorders,* 4th ed. Washington, D.C.: American Psychiatric Association, 1994.

———. *Diagnostic and Statistical Manual of Mental Disorders,* 4th ed. Washington, D.C.: American Psychiatric Association, 2000.

Bryson, Harold T. *The Reality of Hell and the Goodness of God.* Wheaton, IL: Tyndale House Publishers, 1984.

Carlson, Dwight L. *Overcoming Hurts and Anger.* Eugene, OR: Harvest House, 1981.

Cloud, Henry, and John Townsend. *Boundaries.* Grand Rapids, MI: Zondervan, 1992.

Cook, Jeff. *Seven.* Grand Rapids, MI: Zondervan, 2008.

Crabb, Larry. *Shattered Dreams.* Colorado Springs: WaterBrook Press, 2001.

Hales, Robert E., Stuart C. Yudofsky, and John A. Talbott. *Textbook of Psychiatry,* 2nd ed. Washington, D.C.: American Psychiatric

Press, 1994.

Hart, Archibald D. *Adrenaline and Stress*. Nashville, TN: Word Publishing, 1995.

——. *Dark Clouds, Silver Linings*. Colorado Springs: Focus on the Family, 1993.

——. "Personal Health of the Minister." Seminar, Fuller Theological Seminary D. Min Program, Toronto, ON, September 22 1998.

——. *Unmasking Male Depression: Recognizing the Root Cause of Many Problem Behaviors, Such as Anger, Resentment, Abusiveness, Silence, Addictions, and Sexual Compulsiveness*. Nashville, TN: Word Publishing, 2001.

Hazard, David. *Breaking Free from Depression*. Eugene, OR: Harvest House, 2002.

Hennigan, Bruce, and Mark A. Sutton. *Conquering Depression: A 30-day Plan to Finding Happiness*. Nashville, TN: Broadman and Holman Publishers, 2001.

Hensley, J. Clark. *Preacher Behave!* Jackson, MS: Dallas Printing Co., 1985.

Hill, Craig S. *The Ancient Paths*. Littleton, CO: Family Foundations, 1992.

Jamison, Kay Redford. *Night Falls Fast*. New York: Vintage Books, 1999.

Kaplan Harold I., Benjamin J. Sadock, and Jack A. Grebb. "Synopsis of Psychiatry." In *Behavioral Sciences Clinical Psychiatry*. Baltimore, MD: Williams & Wilkins, 1994.

Kollar. Charles Allen. *Solution-Focused Pastoral Counseling*. Grand Rapids, MI: Zondervan, 1997.

LaHaye, Tim, and Bob Phillips. *Anger Is a Choice*. Grand Rapids, MI: Zondervan, 2002.

Mayo Clinic Staff, "Dysthymia." Mayo Foundation for Medical Education and Research, http://www.mayoclinic.com/health/dysthymia/DS01111 (access December 20, 2012)

Mayo Clinic Staff, "Seasonal affective disorder (SAD)." Mayo Foundation for Medical Education and Research, http://www.mayoclinic.com/health/seasonal-affective-disorder/DS00195 (access September 22, 2011).

Mayo Clinic Staff, "Cyclothymia." Mayo Foundation for Medical Education and Research, http://www.mayoclinic.com/health/cyclothymia/DS00729 (access June 13, 2012).

Merriam-Webster, *Webster's II New College Dictionary.* New York: Houghton Mifflin, 2001.

National Institute of Mental Health. *The Numbers Count: Mental Disorders in America.* Bethesda, MD: NIMH Publication # 01-4584, 2005.

———. *Suicide Facts.* NIMH Publication, 1999. Cited by Mental Health Matters http://www.mental-health-matters.com/articles/article.php?artID=390 (accessed March 27, 2006; page now discontinued).

National Strategy for Suicide Prevention. *Suicide: Cost to the Nation.* http:// www.mentalhealth.samhsa.gov/suicideprevention/costtonation.asp (accessed March 27, 2006; page now discontinued).

Nouwen, Henri. *Here and Now.* New York: Crossroads, 1994.

———. *The Inner Voice of Love: A Journey through Anguish to Freedom.* New York: Harper Collins, 1996.

Peterson, Eugene H. *The Message: The Bible in Contemporary Language.* Colorado Springs: Navpress, 2002.

Southgate, Nicole Elizabeth, "Suicide Prevention." Speech, meeting of the Rotary Club, Greer, SC, March 2004.

Smith, Jeffery K. "Mood Disorders." Keynote address, winter board meeting of H.I.M. Ministries, Easley, SC, February 5, 2004.

Tasman Allan, Jerald Kay and Jeffery A. Lieberman. *Psychiatry Therapeutics,* 2d ed. Chichester, West Sussex, England: John Wiley & Sons, 2003.

Warren, Rick, *The Purpose Driven Church.* Grand Rapids, MI: Zondervan, 1995.

Warren, Neil Clark *Make Anger Your Ally.* Wheaton IL: Tyndale House Publishers, 1999.

Westfall, John. *Coloring Outside The Lines.* San Francisco: Harper, 1991.

For more information about
Greg L. Russ
&

HELP! SOMEONE I LOVE IS DEPRESSED
please visit:

www.greglruss.com

....

For more information about
AMBASSADOR INTERNATIONAL
please visit:

www.ambassador-international.com
@AmbassadorIntl
www.facebook.com/AmbassadorIntl